THE CHRISTMAS BOOK

THE CHRISTMAS BOOK

ANNE FARNCOMBE

NATIONAL CHRISTIAN EDUCATION COUNCIL
Robert Denholm House
Nutfield, Redhill, Surrey, RH1 4HW

TO PATRICK
for all his help

First Published 1982

ISBN 0-7197-0343-3
Typeset by Solo Typesetting, Maidstone, Kent
Printed and bound by BPCC-AUP Aberdeen Ltd.

CONTENTS

THE FIRST CHRISTMAS

The story of how Jesus was born in Bethlehem nearly two thousand years ago is recorded in the Bible. This is how it is written in the Good News Bible . . .

od sent the angel Gabriel to a town in Galilee named Nazareth. He had a message for a girl promised in marriage to a man named Joseph, who was a descendant of King David. The girl's name was Mary.

The angel came to her and said, 'Peace be with you! The Lord is with you and has greatly blessed you!'

Mary was deeply troubled by the angel's message, and she wondered what his words meant.

The angel said to her, 'Don't be afraid, Mary; God has been gracious to you. You will become pregnant and give birth to a son, and you will name him Jesus. He will be great and will be called the Son of the Most High God. The Lord God will make him a king, as his ancestor David was, and he will be the king of the descendants of Jacob for ever; his kingdom will never end!'

'I am the Lord's servant,' said Mary; 'may it happen to me as you have said.'

And the angel left her.

Mary said:

My heart praises the Lord; my soul is glad because of God my Saviour, for he has remembered me, his lowly servant! From now on all people will call me happy, because of the great things the Mighty God has done for me. His name is holy; from one generation to another he shows mercy to those who honour him. He has stretched out his mighty arm and scattered the proud with all their plans.

He has brought down mighty kings from their thrones, and lifted up the lowly. He has filled the hungry with good things, and sent the rich away with empty hands. He has kept the promise he made to our ancestors, and has come to the help of his servant Israel. He has remembered to show mercy to Abraham and to all his descendants for ever!

t that time the Emperor Augustus ordered a census to be taken throughout the Roman Empire. When this first census took place, Quirinus was the governor of Syria. Everyone, then, went to register himself, each to his own town.

Joseph went from the town of Nazareth in Galilee to the town of Bethlehem in Judaea, the birthplace of King David. Joseph went there because he was a descendant of David.

He went to register with Mary, who was promised in marriage to him. She was pregnant, and while they were in Bethlehem, the time came for her to have her baby. She gave birth to her first son, wrapped him in strips of cloth and laid him in a manger – there was no room for them to stay in the inn.

here were some shepherds in that part of the country who were spending the night in the fields, taking care of their flocks.

An angel of the Lord appeared to them, and the glory of the Lord shone over them.

They were terribly afraid, but the angel said to them, 'Don't be afraid! I am here with good news for you, which will bring great joy to all the people. This very day in David's town your Saviour was born – Christ the Lord! And this is what will prove it to you: you will find a baby wrapped in strips of cloth and lying in a manger.'

Suddenly a great army of heaven's angels appeared with the angel, singing praises to God:

'Glory to God in the highest heaven, and peace on earth to those with whom he is pleased!'

When the angels went away from them back into heaven, the shepherds said to one another, 'Let's go to Bethlehem and see this thing that has happened, which the Lord has told us.'

So they hurried off and found Mary and Joseph and saw the baby lying in the manger. When the shepherds saw him, they told them what the angel had said about the child. All who heard it were amazed at what the shepherds said.

Mary remembered all these things and thought deeply about them. The shepherds went back, singing praises to God for all they had heard and seen; it had been just as the angel had told them.

esus was born in the town of Bethlehem in Judaea, during the time when Herod was king. Soon afterwards, some men who studied the stars came from the east to Jerusalem and asked, 'Where is the baby born to be the king of the Jews? We saw his star when it came up in the east, and we have come to worship him.'

When King Herod heard about this, he was very upset, and so was everyone else in Jerusalem.

He called together all the chief priests and the teachers of the Law and asked them, 'Where will the Messiah be born?'

'In the town of Bethlehem in Judaea,' they answered. 'For this is what the prophet wrote:

> Bethlehem in the land of Judah,
> you are by no means the least of
> the leading cities of Judah;
> for from you will come a leader
> who will guide my people Israel.

So Herod called the visitors from the east to a secret meeting and found out from them the exact time the star had appeared. Then he sent them to Bethlehem with these instructions: 'Go and make a careful search for the child, and when you find him, let me know, so that I too may go and worship him.'

And so they left, and on their way they saw the same star they had seen in the east. When they saw it, how happy they were, and what joy was theirs! It went ahead of them until it stopped over the place where the child was.

They went into the house, and when they saw the child with his mother Mary, they knelt down and worshipped him. They brought out their gifts of gold, frankincense, and myrrh, and presented them to him.

Then they returned to their country by another road, since God had warned them in a dream not to go back to Herod.

This story is quoted from the Good News Bible: Luke 1.16-33, 38, 46-55; Luke 2.1-20; Matthew 2.1-12.

WHERE JESUS WAS BORN

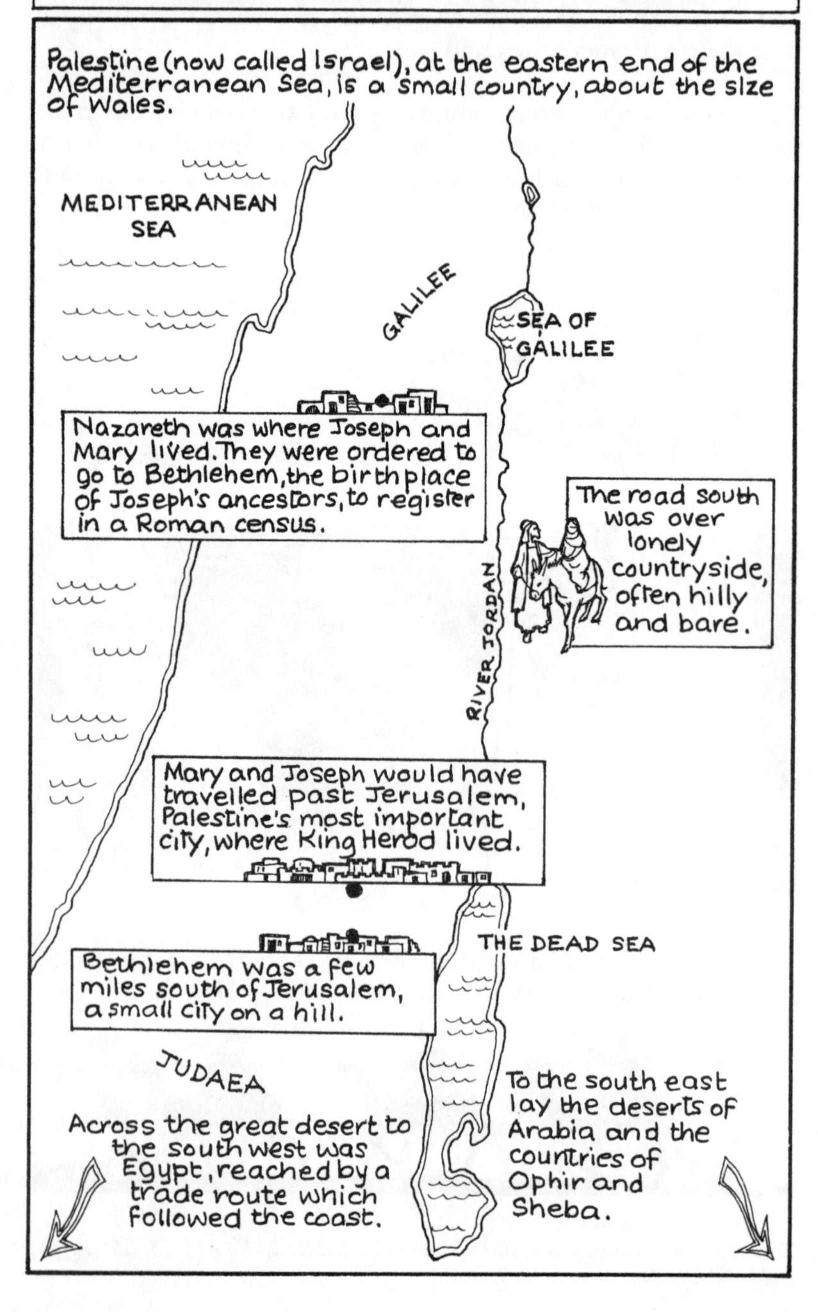

LIFE IN PALESTINE when Jesus was born

About sixty years before Jesus was born, Palestine had been made part of the Roman province of Syria and was an enemy occupied country.

Roman standards were raised on public buildings and in the streets. Roman soldiers were garrisoned in the chief towns. It was their job to control the Jewish people, maintain and guard the trade routes, and force the people to pay taxes to Rome.

The Romans, however, did leave the Jewish people to worship as they wanted to. They were allowed to hold services in the synagogues and in the temple at Jerusalem.

Roman standard

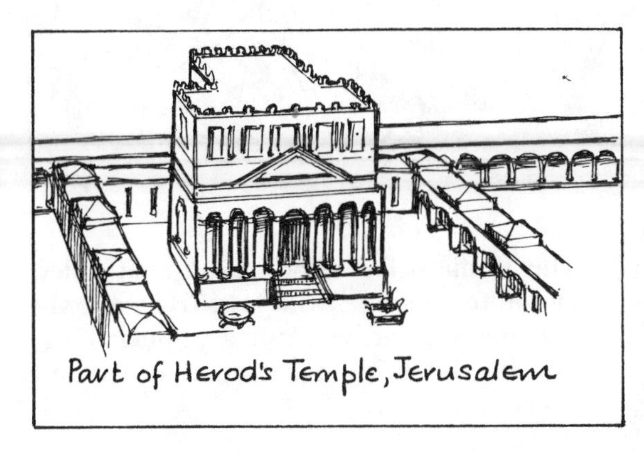

Part of Herod's Temple, Jerusalem

At the time when Jesus was born, Augustus was the Emperor of Rome.

The Emperor Augustus wanted to know exactly how many people he had in his large empire. This would tell him how much money he could expect to receive from the taxes they paid.

He ordered a widespread census. For this, every man had to register in the town or city where he had been born.

Hundreds of families travelled many miles, mainly on foot, to go back to their ancestral homes.

The Romans had appointed a man called Herod to be king of the Jews. He was only half-Jewish, and was not a popular king, but he did help to maintain order and peace.

King Herod was sly and ruthless, and very anxious to keep his kingdom.

Because Joseph's family had come from Bethlehem, he had to travel there, with Mary, from their home in Nazareth.

Bethlehem was crowded with visitors who had arrived for the census.

The inn at Bethlehem was completely full. Most inns in those days were built round a courtyard. The travellers' donkeys were housed in rough stables on the ground floor, along with the cattle and goats. Above the stables were rooms where the travellers could sleep.

Mary and Joseph were probably glad to be offered shelter in one of these stables. They needed warmth and privacy, as Mary's baby was about to be born.

In the stables there would have been dry hay, and a manger, which was a feeding trough for the animals. Mangers were often made of rough hollowed stone.

When Mary's baby had been born, he would be washed, and then wrapped in a square of cloth. This was then bound round with long strips of cotton cloth. Sometimes these long cloths are known as swaddling clothes.

Jewish women believed that the strips of cloth, wound tightly round the baby's body, would help the little limbs to grow straight and strong.

Out in the fields which stretched below the town of Bethlehem shepherds guarded their sheep from thieves and wild animals.

The Bible records that the shepherds were the first people to be told that a saviour for the Jews had been born.

Jewish people were taught that one day a MESSIAH, or saviour, would come to deliver them from their enemies. They believed that he would rule Israel.

Later, important men from countries to the east of Palestine came looking for this new ruler.

They were astrologers, men who studied the stars and found hidden meanings in them. Seeing an unusually bright light in the sky, they were certain that it meant that a great person was about to be born.

News had reached them that the Jewish people in Palestine were hoping for a new ruler, perhaps a king, who would rise up and overthrow the Romans. Perhaps, they thought, this particularly bright star was his sign.

Naturally, the wise men expected the new ruler to be born in the capital of Palestine, Jerusalem, so they went to Herod's palace.

Herod the Great was very interested. The astrologers had brought rich gifts for the new king, but Herod did not know anything about him. He asked his own learned advisers if they knew anything about a forecast of a new king.

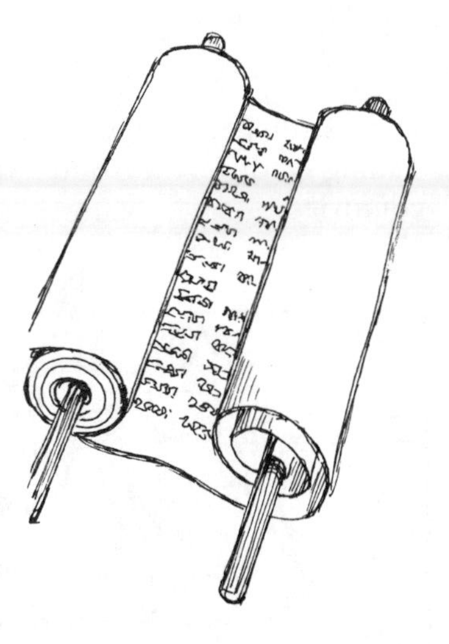

'Yes,' they said. 'It is prophesied that he will be born in King David's city, Bethlehem.'

King Herod sent the wise men on a few miles to Bethlehem, asking them to report back to him with news.

In Bethlehem, where Mary and Joseph were probably living in a house by now, the wise men found the new king. They offered him their gifts.

They gave him gold; it could have been mined in Ophir, or in Sheba in western Arabia. This was a gift of wealth suitable for any king!

They gave him frankincense. This was a valuable resin that people had learnt to extract from the bark of a tree. When burnt, this gum gave off a sweet smell, and was used by the Jews in worship.

They gave him myrrh. This was another resin, sweet-smelling and expensive. It was known to relieve pain, and was used when preparing a body for burial.

The astrologers did not go back to King Herod in Jerusalem. Taking a different route, they travelled home to their own countries.

ADVENT

Advent is the season observed by the Church in the weeks leading up to Christmas, and it marks the beginning of the Church's year.

The word ADVENT comes from two Latin words meaning coming towards. The four weeks leading up to Christmas are called Advent because they are a time when people are preparing for the greatest 'coming' of all time – the birth of Jesus Christ.

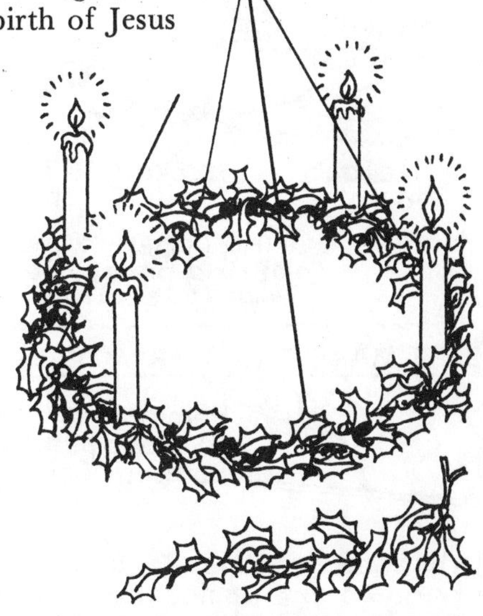

One of the most popular customs of Advent began in Scandinavian countries. A wreath is made by twisting evergreens round a wire hoop. At equal distances round the wreath, four candles are fixed, and the wreath is hung in the church. Advent wreaths are sometimes hung in homes and schools.

The first candle is lit on the first Sunday in Advent. On the second Sunday it is lit again, and a second one with it. By the fourth Sunday, all the candles have been lit, and on Christmas Eve it is taken down. A Christmas crib often replaces it, showing that Christmas has really arrived.

Have a look for Advent wreaths in churches at Christmas time. It might be too much of a fire risk to make one for your own home but, if you can borrow four small battery torches, you may be able to construct your own wreath using them.

ADVENT CALENDAR MOBILE

Once December has arrived, it can seem a long wait during Advent until it is December 25th, Christmas Day. Make this Advent Calendar mobile, then add a picture a day from December 1st. It will make an extra decoration for your room, too.

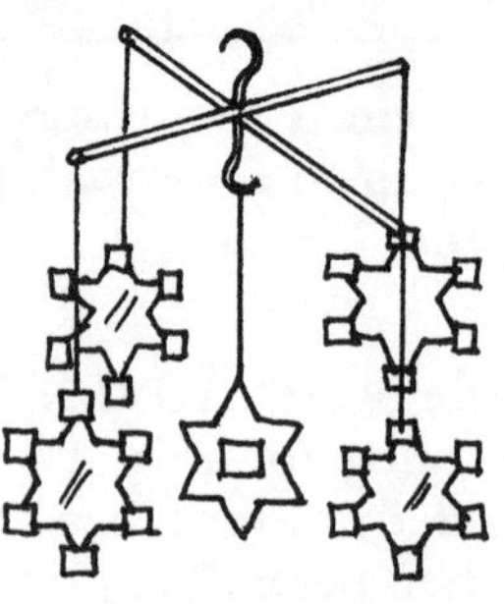

YOU WILL NEED:

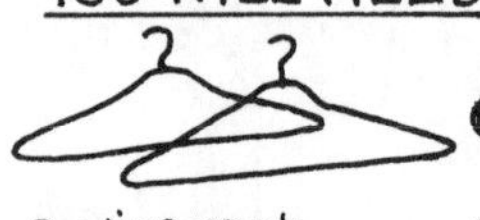

2 wire coat hangers

cooking foil

strong thin wire

cotton

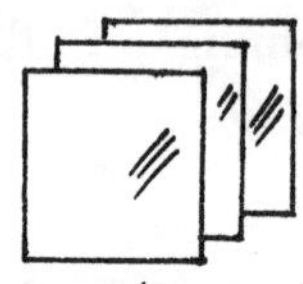

cardboard or stiff foil

and:- tracing paper; drawing paper; colouring pens or pencils; scissors; sellotape.

TO MAKE THE 'STAR-MOBILE':

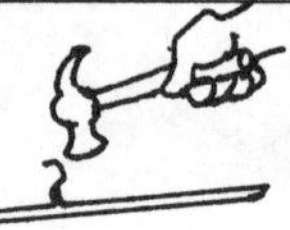

Hammer both coat-hangers into long thin shapes. Cover each with cooking foil.

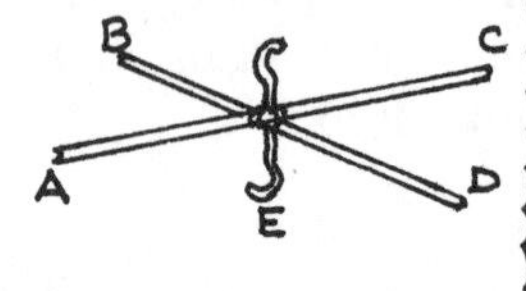

Put them together to form a cross, hanging one upside-down under the other. Tie them together in the centre with wire.

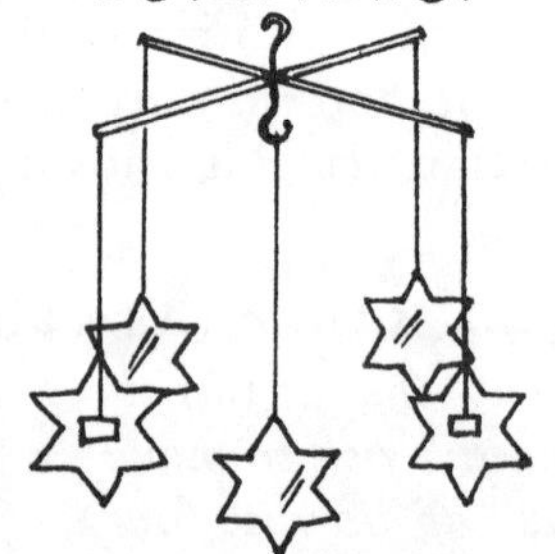

Attach lengths of cotton (about 30 cms (12 ins) long), to points A, B, C, D and E.
Using the star template on page 125, cut 5 stars from the cardboard or stiff foil.
With cellotape, stick one star firmly on the end of each length of cotton.

If possible, finish this part of your Advent Calendar mobile BEFORE THE END OF NOVEMBER.

(Continued at foot of next page)

CHRISTMAS TREE ADVENT CALENDAR

(Use the small pictures on pages 24 and 25 for both Advent calendars.)

Enlarge this drawing of a Christmas tree, (see page 127), on to a piece of A4 paper (21 x 29·8 cms or $8\frac{1}{4}$ x $11\frac{3}{4}$ ins). Stiffen it by sticking it to cardboard. When the glue is dry colour the picture with paint or felt-tip pens. Write on the numbers where shown. Try to complete this part of the calendar by November 30th.

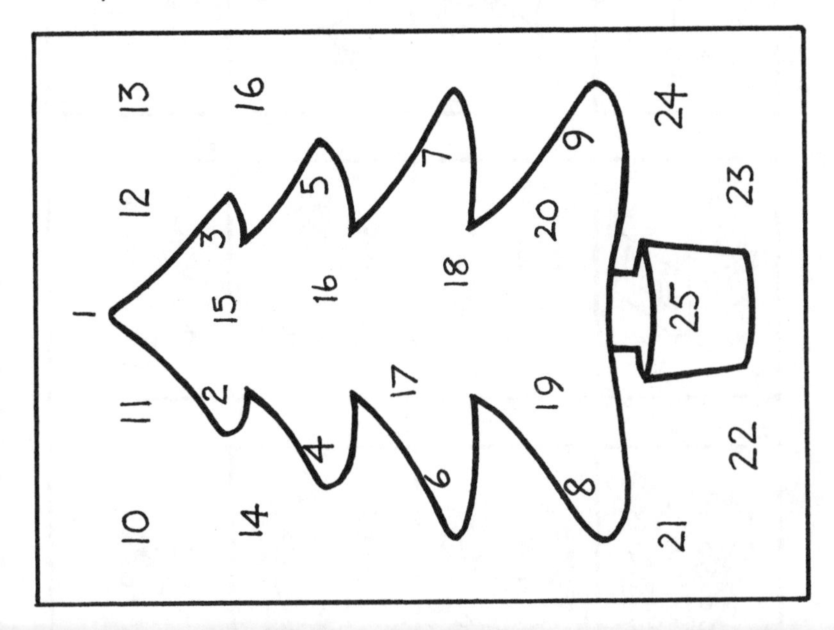

For either calendar:

Each day, beginning on December 1st, trace, colour and cut out one of the small pictures, beginning with number 1.

For star-mobile Advent calendar:

Stick one picture a day on to one of the points on any star hanging from A, B, C or D. The last picture, No. 25, is larger. Trace and colour this on Christmas Eve, so that you can stick it to the centre of the star hanging from E on Christmas morning. The instructions for the Christmas tree calendar are overleaf.

For Christmas Tree Advent calendar:

Stick one picture a day on to the numbered places on the tree. When the last picture is attached on Christmas morning your Christmas tree will be fully decorated!

★ Each picture has some connection with the Christmas season. After tracing them, colour them as brightly as you can, so that they can be seen clearly by all the family. Cut out each square. ★

Instructions for making the Advent calendars are given on pages 22 and 23.

CHRISTMAS IS HERE!

Long before Christians began to celebrate the birth of Christ, there were pagan festivals held in mid-December.

December 21 is the shortest day of the year, when the nights are long and darkness comes early. After that date the hours of day-light increase and the turning-point of winter is past. This time is called the winter solstice. The Romans celebrated the turning year with feasts and present giving.

At the same time of the year, in the colder parts of Europe, similar customs were held to celebrate the continuance of life, the hope of spring returning. This Celtic feast was called JUUL which, in English, became YULE.

When Christians began to think about celebrating the birth of Christ, particularly with a special communion service, or mass, they also chose mid-winter. It would be easier, they thought, for those who were used to celebrating the winter solstice. Instead of feasting the return of spring, they could feast the birth of Jesus Christ. There is a record that the English word *Christmas* was first used in an Anglo-Saxon chronicle. Most churches decided that December 25 should be Christ's official feast day. So Christ's mass became CHRISTMAS.

CHRISTMAS GREETINGS

We say 'A happy Christmas!' or 'Merry Christmas!' to our friends at Christmas time. Here are greetings used in some other countries.

YULE-TIDE CUSTOMS

Christmas, in very early days, was often still called yuletide.

The bringing in of the yule log was once the most important custom in many countries. The log was usually cut from an oak, ash or apple tree.

The log was lit on Christmas Eve and burnt on an open hearth. Superstitions surrounded the ceremony. If the log went out, or burnt too quickly, it was a bad omen for the people living in the house. It had to burn for at least twelve hours, and preferably for several days, but it had to be extinguished by the twelfth day of Christmas, January 6.

The yule log was dragged to the house from the place where it was cut. Sometimes a horse was needed to pull it. It was decorated with evergreens, and sometimes ribbons, and taken home with great merriment.

The yule candle was large and specially made. Often it was coloured, and decorated with holly.

The candle was usually lit on Christmas Eve, and had to burn all through the night.

The last little bit of candle was treasured all through the year. People thought it would give them protection against bad luck.

A proper yule candle is hardly ever seen now, although candles themselves are often a part of our Christmas decorations. Have you noticed how many times they are pictured on Christmas cards?

Some people say that Martin Luther, the German preacher, first put candles on Christmas trees. He thought they would remind people of the Christmas star.

In some places candles are put in the windows of houses, and lit when darkness comes. This comes from an old belief that the Christ-child, wandering in the winter cold, will be guided by the candle's light to the warmth and welcome of a friendly house.

A LEGEND FROM SAXON TIMES

One Christmas Eve the people in the village were already celebrating Christmas with feasting and singing.

The Saxon priest, Eddy, was preparing to hold a midnight service in the church. He set out with his lantern and entered the dark building. Lighting the altar candles, he could just make out the rough stone walls, and the uneven earth floor where the people would stand to listen while he preached to them God's good news of Christmas.

Just before midnight he rang the bell and waited for the people to arrive. He could hear them singing and shouting outside in the darkness, but no one came into the little church.

Eddy wondered what to do. Then the church door creaked open. 'At last,' thought the priest, and turned to greet his congregation.

In the half-light he could make out a strange form, something with a large head, four legs, and two long ears! In front of him stood a donkey, its head bowed low. Soon a young bullock followed the donkey and stood beside it in front of the altar.

'Well, at least they will listen to me,' thought Eddy, and began the service. He found his thoughts were not about the people still feasting and singing outside in the darkness, but of a lonely stable where Jesus was born, with animals such as these for company. And as he preached to them in the candlelight, telling them the story of the first Christmas, neither animal moved at all.

WASSAILING – AN OLD CUSTOM

The custom of wassailing began in Saxon times. Wassails were songs which were a mixture of seasonal good wishes and begging.

At Christmas time, the lord of the manor house called together his whole household. Everyone drank hot ale from a large wooden bowl, known as the wassail bowl.

Later, when people had their own village cottages and no longer lived in the manor house or its grounds, they still kept up the wassailing custom.

They went out after dark, carrying an empty wooden or earthenware cup decorated with ribbons and evergreens. They went to the houses of wealthy people and sang songs outside. The cup was presented to the householder, who was expected to fill it with wine or food. It was known as the wassail cup.

Nearly all wassailing songs mentioned items that the singers would like to be given by the wealthy people. So one song would have a verse which included 'good loaf and cheese', and another 'a good piece of beef'. As the singers were presented with gifts, they would stand and drink the health of the household.

Here are some words of two very old wassailing songs.

TRADITIONAL CHRISTMAS FOOD

If you had lived in the time of Queen Elizabeth I, you would have had an enormous feast at Christmas.

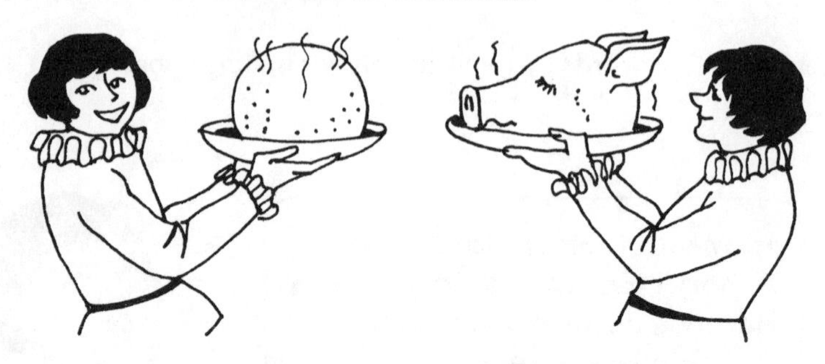

You would have *started* your meal with Christmas pudding, but a very different one from the kind we know today.

It was a mixture, rather like porridge, made with oatmeal, meat broth, breadcrumbs, dried fruit and spice.

The pudding was often eaten *with* the meat, which was usually roast boar's head. Boars were wild, and were hunted as a sport.

After the pudding and the boar's head, you would have eaten:

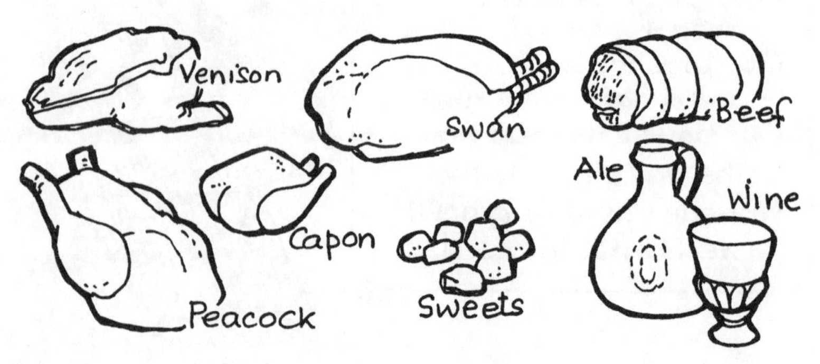

Later, in the 17th century, the Puritans ruled our country for a time.

They tried to abolish Christmas altogether! Parliament made laws which forbad feasting and celebration. The laws even ordered people to fast on Christmas Day.

The people were very angry, and there were demonstrations and rioting. There was harsh punishment for law-breakers.

When at last a king ruled England again, Christmas came back. But never again did the people eat quite as much as they had done in Elizabethan days.

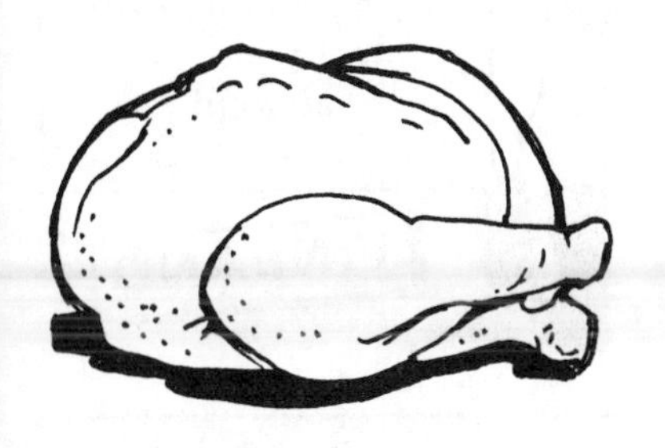

The Christmas pudding was now made with dried plums (prunes) and was called a plum pudding. It was boiled in a cloth, and eaten after the meat dish. Turkeys, which were introduced from America, and beef replaced the boar's head.

Make a list of the ingredients used in today's Christmas puddings.

Not all countries eat turkey and Christmas pudding for their Christmas meal. Many places have their own traditional food.

Christmas Eve

Almond Soup
Chicken
or turkey
Turrone
(a kind of
nougat)

SPAIN

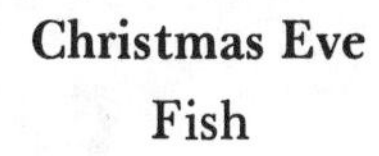

Christmas Eve

Fish

Christmas Day

Ravioli
Roast guinea-fowl
or boiled capon
with cheese and
herb stuffing

ITALY

SWEDEN

Christmas Eve

Cold ham, spare ribs,
herrings
Apples, prunes
Marzipan tarts filled
with cloudberries
(like blackberries)

Christmas Day

Lufti – dried fish
with white sauce

CZECHO-SLOVAKIA

Christmas Eve

Pea or bean soup
Fish
Potato salad
Chocolates
Nuts

Write your own Christmas menu here

Beach Picnic

Cold turkey
Salad
Hot plum pudding

AUSTRALIA

Most countries cook special Christmas

CAKES

In GREECE a very elaborate cake is made. It is called CHRISTOPSOMO-'Christ Bread'.

In ROUMANIA the cake at Christmas is shaped like the folds of swaddling clothes

In ITALY a dome-shaped, very light cake full of candied fruit is baked. It is called PANETTONE.

This recipe for Christmas tea biscuits comes from GREECE. TRY IT!

In GERMANY four cakes are made to be eaten on the four Sundays in Advent

75g (or 3oz) sugar
75g (or 3oz) margarine
1 egg
200g (or 8oz) plain flour
75g (or 3oz) raisins
½ teasp nutmeg
½ teasp cinnamon
½ teasp bicarb soda

Melt sugar and margarine in a saucepan. Cool slightly and beat in the egg. Add sifted flour, nutmeg, cinnamon, bicarb soda and raisins. With floured hands, roll into balls about 4cm (1½ ins) diameter. Place on greased baking tin. Bake in a moderate oven (Regulo 4, 350°F, 175°C) for 15-20 minutes. When cool, halve and spread with butter.

MINCE PIES

Mincemeat is a traditional filling for pastry tarts at Christmas time. It is made from lots of dried fruit (raisins, sultanas and currants), and sugar, suet and spices.

Long ago, mince pies were made with minced lamb or mutton, with dried fruit and spices. They were not round, as they usually are today, but boat-shaped, or oval. Some people say that they were made this shape to remind everyone of the manger in which Jesus was laid.

We no longer put minced meat into our mince pies, but we put in animal fat – suet.

Even when mince pies were made from lamb or mutton, people said that each pie meant a happy month.

When we buy mincemeat, it has not been cooked. All the ingredients are mixed thoroughly and put into jars or tins. Alcohol is usually added in small quantities, and this helps to keep the mincemeat fresh for a long time.

CHRISTMAS PRESENTS

Long before the Christian festival of Christmas, people used to give each other gifts in mid-winter. In ancient Rome, during the winter Saturnalia celebrations, wealthy people gave money, food and clothes to the poorer people who lived nearby.

Christians kept up this mid-winter giving to celebrate what was a very happy time of year for them. Giving presents reminds Christians of God's gift of his Son, Jesus, and of the first gifts given to the baby by the wise men.

In 1647, when Christmas was abolished by the Puritans, all the shops were open on 25 December, and the churches closed. Thirteen years later, King Charles II came to the throne, and Christmas came back; the people could celebrate again. But many of the old customs and traditions were forgotten, for the people had become used to the strict rules of the Puritans.

It was not until Queen Victoria ruled, nearly two hundred years later, that people began to look back on the good old days of the past, and many old customs were revived.

Back came the lavish Christmas feasts, the gaudy decorations, the singing and the dancing, and the elaborate present giving.

If you had lived in Victorian times, you might have chosen these presents to give to the members of your family:

From your Victorian parents, if they were wealthy, you could expect to receive something like this:

a lovely French doll, or a model sailing ship—

—a musical pig

— or an elephant on wheels, to ride on!

In Victorian days people were either rich or very, very poor. Not many people were 'in between'. If you belonged to a poor family you would probably have had no money to buy Christmas gifts. But you would still have given presents if you could, and you would have made your own.

Girls liked to sew samplers, and might have made one something like this to give away:

Other children would spend many secret hours making up poetry, then write their poem out carefully and give it to someone. Some of the poems were very sentimental, and often tragic, as this one looks as though it will be:

I tell you a story sad, of one
Who was known as little Beth;
The roses had faded, winter had come,
And the child was near to death....

These home-made Christmas gifts would be treasured for many years, long after more expensive ones had been forgotten.

Today, present-giving is still a very important part of Christmas. As early as August some shops advertise their Christmas stocks, and usually by the beginning of November decorations are in the shop windows.

Think back over the Christmases you have had. Can you remember one present that gave you more pleasure than any other? Ask older people if they can remember any special ones, too.

You can be sure that your parents or grandparents still treasure some of the presents they have received from you, especially any that you have taken the trouble to make yourself.

Here, and on the next few pages, are suggestions for a few gifts that you could make very cheaply.

This pincushion is in the shape and style of one made by Victorian children.

Using this shape as a template, cut two fish shapes out of felt or other thick material. Use a felt-tip pen to draw on the eyes and scales, and let the ink dry thoroughly.

Trying to use very small stitches, sew the two fish-shaped pieces of felt together, leaving a gap as shown.

Stuff the fish through the gap with kapok, cotton wool, or old nylon tights, cut into narrow strips.

On the back of the fish sew a piece of elastic at A and B. When the dressmaker is using the pins she can slip her hand through the elastic, and wear the pin-cushion on her wrist. If she does this, the pin-cushion cannot be put down and mis-laid!

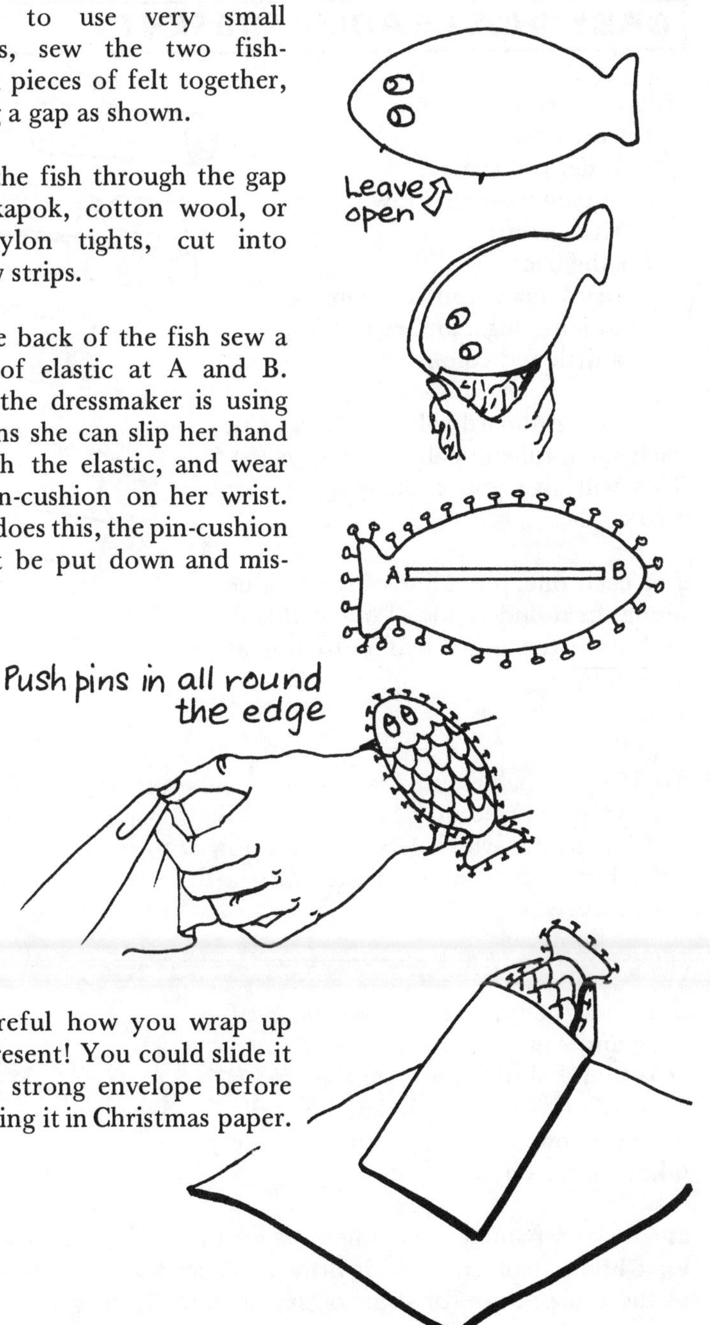

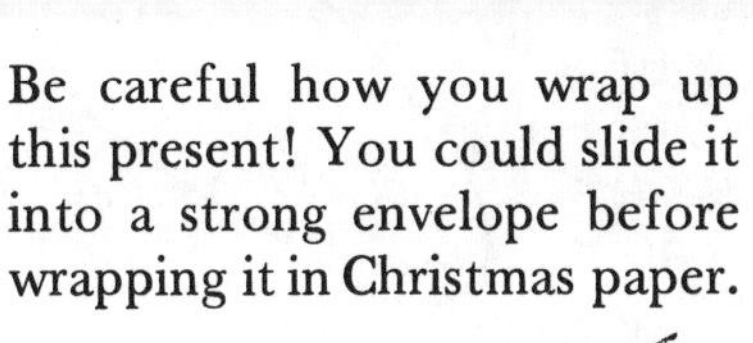

Be careful how you wrap up this present! You could slide it into a strong envelope before wrapping it in Christmas paper.

BABY IN A CRADLE PRESENT

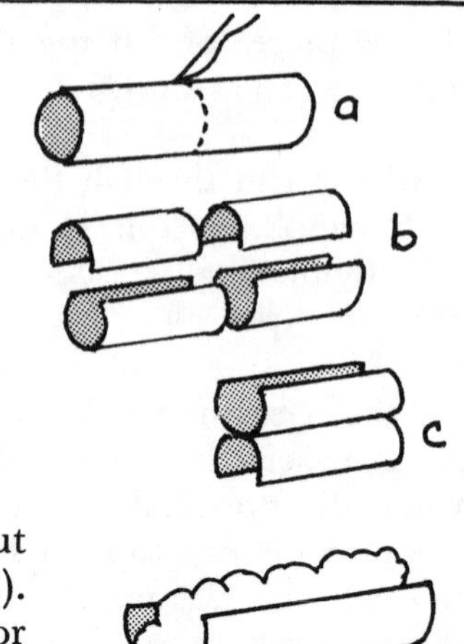

You will need:
for the cradle –
toilet roll centre,
cotton wool or straw,
glue, paint;
for the baby –
ready-made fondant icing,
or icing sugar and egg white,
a little red colouring.

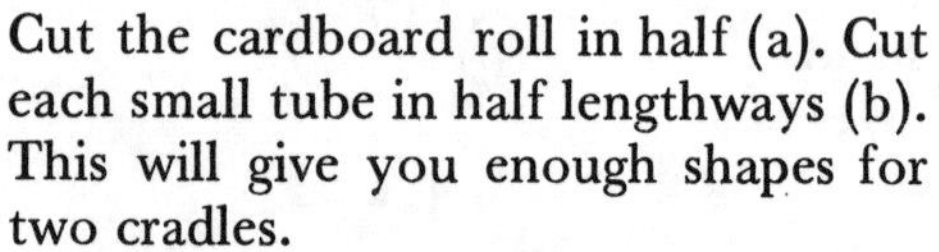

Cut the cardboard roll in half (a). Cut each small tube in half lengthways (b). This will give you enough shapes for two cradles.

For each one, put a line of strong glue along the rounded side of one half-roll, and stick the other half onto this as shown (c).

To make the babies, use ready-made fondant icing, or make your own icing. Sift about 75g (or 3oz) icing sugar into a bowl and add a little egg white. Mix with a spoon or fork until you have a stiff, but not crumbly, paste. Add a little more egg white if necessary.

For each baby, use a small piece of icing and roll it into the shape shown at (d), and about the same size. Keep some of the icing to use later. Put the babies on one side to dry out; this may take about an hour.

Meanwhile, paint your cradle pink or blue or, if you want it to look like a manger, paint it brown. When dry, lay cotton wool in the top portion (or straw or dry grass for a manger) as shown in (e).

When the icing baby is dry, add a tiny amount of red colouring to the icing you have left. Form a little of this pink paste into a small ball (f) for the baby's face. Place it on one end of the baby, and press gently to flatten (g). If it does not stick easily, moisten the white icing with a drop of water and press again. Mark the eyes, nose and mouth with a skewer or thin knitting needle, making sure the eyes are drawn half-way down the face (h).

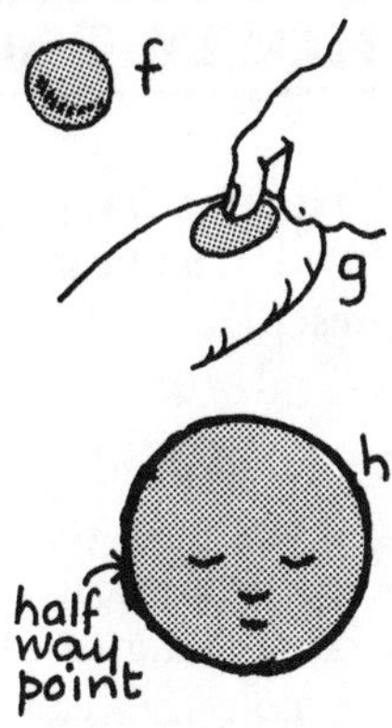

When the whole baby has dried out completely, place it in the cradle.

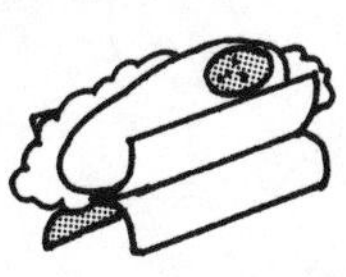

To wrap a present like this, you will need a large piece of wrapping paper, at least 40cms (or 16 ins) square.

HOLLY CANDLESTICK

Adapt the hanging holly ball (see page 93) to make a candle holder for a present.

You will need:
- a large potato (scrubbed clean),
- sprigs of holly,
- short lengths of ivy,
- a coloured candle,
- knife, cooking foil.

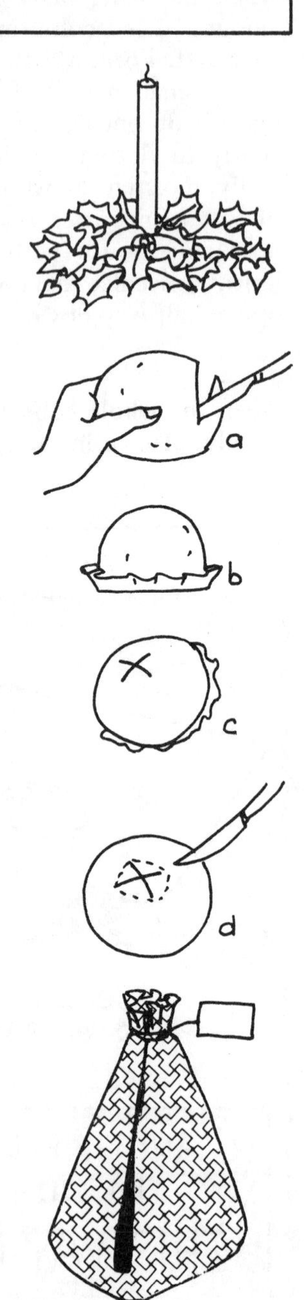

Cut a slice off the bottom of the potato so that it will stand (a). Dry the cut end with kitchen paper or blotting paper.

Cut a piece of kitchen foil slightly larger than the cut end, and wrap it round as shown (b).

Cut a cross in the top of the potato (c) and ease out a hole a little smaller than the candle end, and about 1.5cms (or ¾ ins) deep (d). Wrap the end of the candle in a small piece of foil, and press into the hole in the potato.

Cover the potato by sticking in holly and ivy (see page 93).

Wrap this present following the instructions given on page 47 for the baby in the cradle, but using a larger piece of wrapping paper.

CHRISTMAS CAROLS

Songs have always been sung at Christmas time, but at first the words were usually in Latin, which only the priests understood. Some people say that it was St Francis, in Italy, who was the first person to bring carols to the people in a language they could understand. After a service he held to remind people of the first Christmas, they went home singing the carols they had heard.

The beginnings of the actual word carol are not known, but we do know that when the word was first used it meant a 'dance in a ring'. A group of people formed a ring and while they danced round they sang songs. Usually these songs were sung on the shortest day of the year, December 21. When Christianity spread, the carols became special songs to celebrate the birth of Jesus.

After that, it was the custom for December 21, which was also St Thomas' Day, to begin the carol season. At any time between then and 9 o'clock on Christmas morning, carols could be sung.

At first each county had its own traditional carols, which were learnt by heart as the common people could not read. These regional carols were known as CURLS. Groups of singers went round to the houses in towns and villages in their county to sing their curls. They programmed their singing so that they arrived at a large, rich family home just when they needed food and drink!

Later, as well as carolling to householders, the singers formed groups to sing in the market places and town squares. Instead of food and drink, they were given money by the listeners.

Today carols are sung in many places. You may have a carol service, or concert, in your school. Many churches have them too. A service which is widely held is the service of *Nine Lessons and Carols*. The lessons are Bible readings which tell of the coming of Jesus, and are read between carols. Perhaps you have been to such a service.

Carol singers also go from door to door, or sing in groups at street corners. Usually any money they may collect is given to charity.

Many of the carols we sing today are very old, and the authors and tune writers unknown or forgotten. These medieval songs were written to tell the Christmas story to people who could neither read nor write. Two of them that we still sing today are *God rest you merry, gentlemen*, and *The first Nowell*.

Some of the carols that we sing are more recent, though, and we know a little about how they came to be written.

Hark! the herald angels sing

William Cummings had once been a choirboy in a choir conducted by the great musician Mendelssohn, and he became very fond of the composer's music. He particularly liked one chorus, and wanted to make it into a Christmas hymn. Mendelssohn protested that the chorus was too soldier-like, and not really suitable for church music. But William Cummings went ahead, finding the words for it from some written by Charles Wesley, and some from two other hymn-writers.

Once in royal David's city

This carol always begins the well-known service of *Nine Lessons and Carols* held every year in King's College, Cambridge. The words were written by Mrs C.F.Alexander, who was the wife of an Irish archbishop. The tune was composed by Henry Gauntlett to fit the words. Mrs Alexander also wrote the words of *All things bright and beautiful*.

Silent night, holy night

In the early nineteenth century, everyone looked forward to the special Christmas Eve midnight services. They were the most important part of Christmas.

In Austria, the organist of a little church set off through the snow to practise the hymns he was to play at the midnight service on Christmas Eve in 1818. But he found that the organ had been damaged, probably by mice, and could not be played. It was impossible to mend it in time for the evening service.

The organist, Franz Gruber, did not know what to do. He discussed it with Joseph Mohr, the assistant priest of the church. The priest showed Mr Gruber the words of a simple Christmas poem he had written. Perhaps Mr Gruber could write a tune for it very quickly, and the choir could learn it in time to sing at the midnight mass. The singing could be accompanied by a guitar.

Mr Gruber hurried home to see what he could do. Before long he had composed a lullaby tune to fit the words. The choir was brought together that afternoon to rehearse the words, and it was sung at the midnight service for the first time.

Afterwards, the words and music were put away and it was not until about 45 years later that the hymn became well known. Now it is one of the best-loved lullabies sung at Christmas time.

O come, all ye faithful

This carol was first written in Latin, and called *Adeste Fideles*. It is believed that words and music were both written by John Francis Wade, who lived at the Catholic centre of Douai in France. The carol was translated into English about a hundred years later. One of the verses is sometimes still sung in Latin.

Away in a manger

This carol came to us by a long route. In the mid-nineteenth century many Europeans went to settle in the United States of America, believing they would find fortune there. They took with them many of their old traditions, some of them connected with Christmas. The singing of carols was one of these traditions. Soon the Americans had adapted many of the old European carols, translating them into the English language. No one is sure where the words of *Away in a manger* originated, although some people once thought they had been written by Martin Luther for his own children. A gospel-song writer from Philadelphia, William Kirkpatrick, wrote the tune that we know today.

Here are some new carols for Christmas.

The words for this tune are on the opposite page.

BIRCHTREE

Roy Chapman © 1982

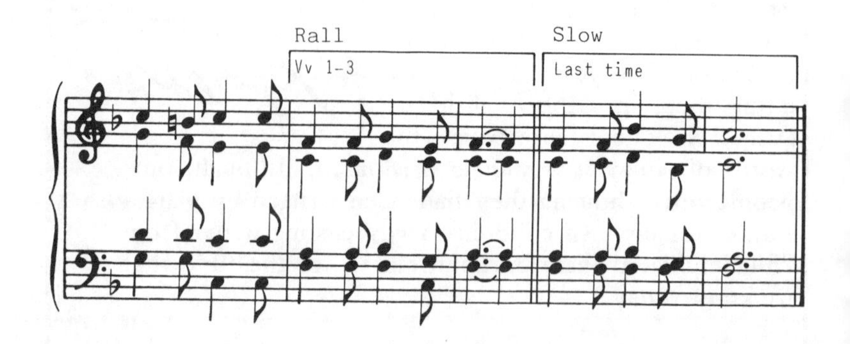

NEW-BORN KING

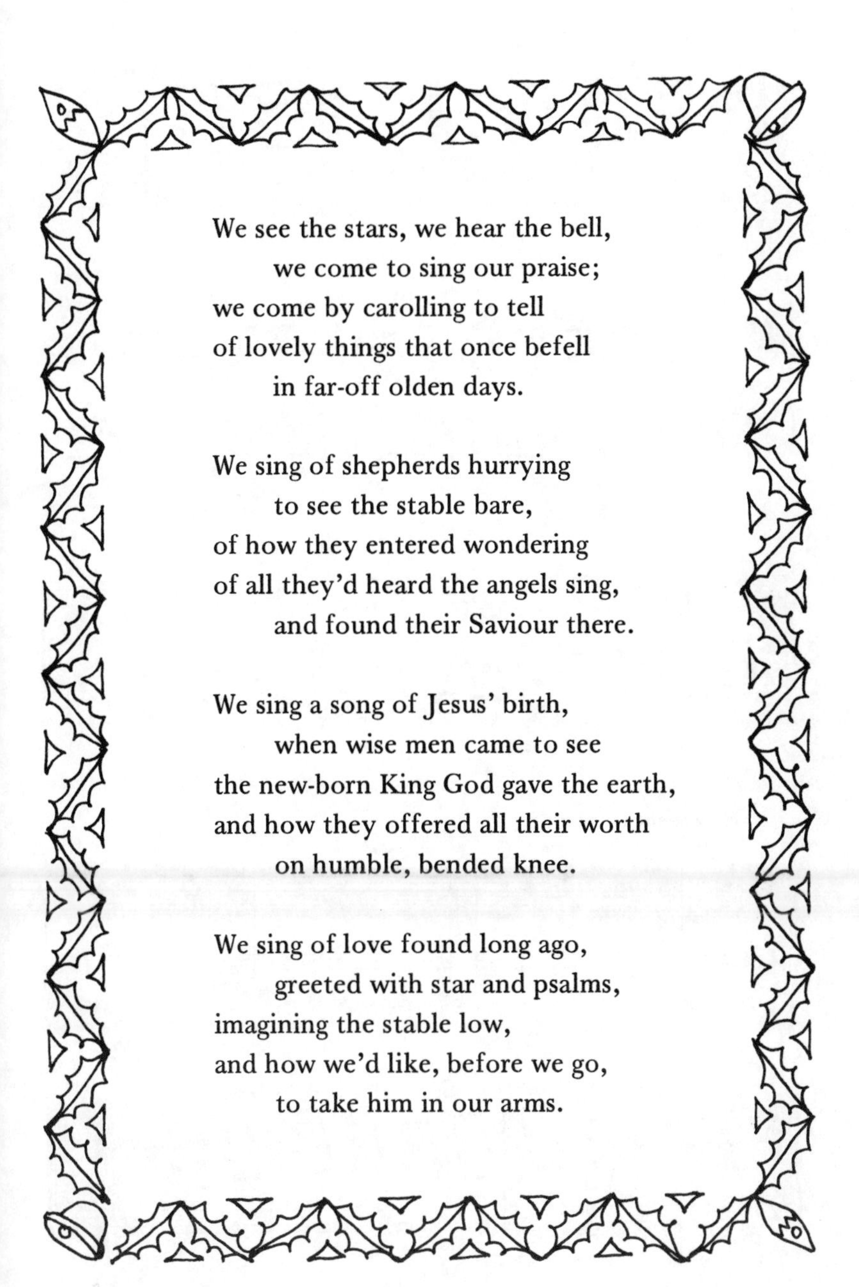

We see the stars, we hear the bell,
we come to sing our praise;
we come by carolling to tell
of lovely things that once befell
in far-off olden days.

We sing of shepherds hurrying
to see the stable bare,
of how they entered wondering
of all they'd heard the angels sing,
and found their Saviour there.

We sing a song of Jesus' birth,
when wise men came to see
the new-born King God gave the earth,
and how they offered all their worth
on humble, bended knee.

We sing of love found long ago,
greeted with star and psalms,
imagining the stable low,
and how we'd like, before we go,
to take him in our arms.

HAMPTON BELLS

Roy Chapman © 1981

SEVEN CHRISTMAS CARDS

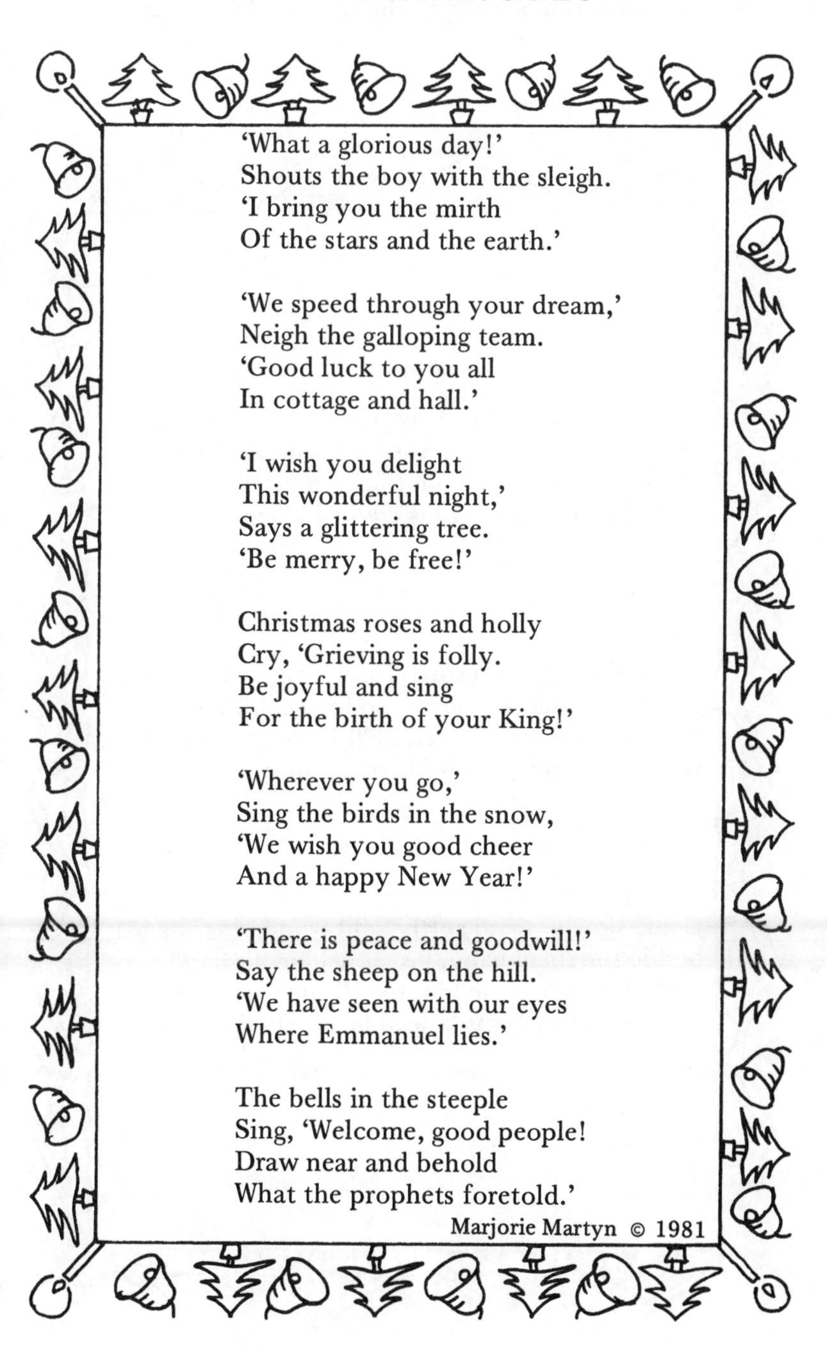

'What a glorious day!'
Shouts the boy with the sleigh.
'I bring you the mirth
Of the stars and the earth.'

'We speed through your dream,'
Neigh the galloping team.
'Good luck to you all
In cottage and hall.'

'I wish you delight
This wonderful night,'
Says a glittering tree.
'Be merry, be free!'

Christmas roses and holly
Cry, 'Grieving is folly.
Be joyful and sing
For the birth of your King!'

'Wherever you go,'
Sing the birds in the snow,
'We wish you good cheer
And a happy New Year!'

'There is peace and goodwill!'
Say the sheep on the hill.
'We have seen with our eyes
Where Emmanuel lies.'

The bells in the steeple
Sing, 'Welcome, good people!
Draw near and behold
What the prophets foretold.'

Marjorie Martyn © 1981

This new carol can be sung to the tune of *Away in a manger.*

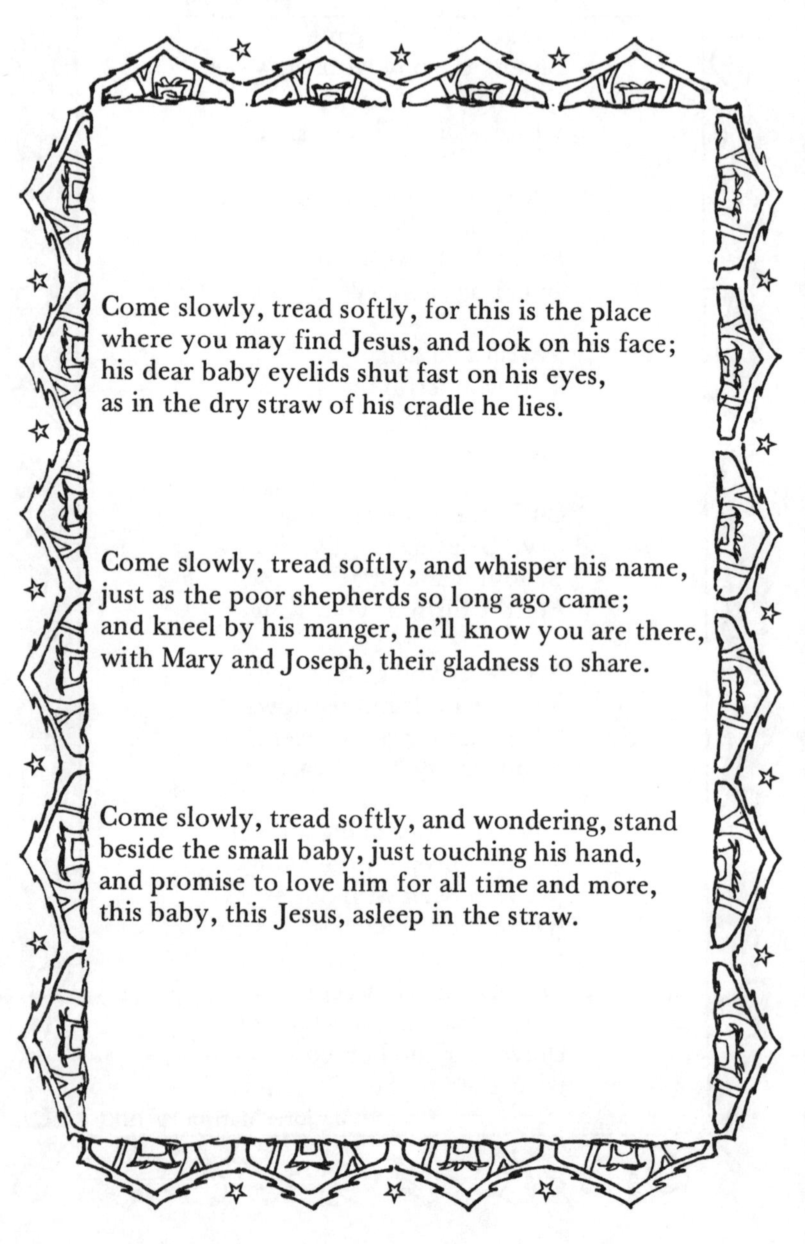

Come slowly, tread softly, for this is the place
where you may find Jesus, and look on his face;
his dear baby eyelids shut fast on his eyes,
as in the dry straw of his cradle he lies.

Come slowly, tread softly, and whisper his name,
just as the poor shepherds so long ago came;
and kneel by his manger, he'll know you are there,
with Mary and Joseph, their gladness to share.

Come slowly, tread softly, and wondering, stand
beside the small baby, just touching his hand,
and promise to love him for all time and more,
this baby, this Jesus, asleep in the straw.

This new carol can be sung to the tune of *O little town of Bethlehem.*

I saw a donkey on the road
Clip-clopping down the hill
from Nazareth to Bethlehem –
the countryside was still;
the donkey had a gentle step
as he was led along,
and Joseph talked with Mary fair
throughout the journey long.

At last they reached the busy town
where they should be next day,
so many people gathered there,
they found no place to stay;
there was no room in house or inn
for Mary's mattress bed,
a stable had to be the place
where she must lay her head.

And then the angels sang their song,
God's greatest news to bring,
of peace on earth that starry night,
and of a new-born king.
While Mary cradled, in her joy,
her baby, her delight,
the stable seemed to glow with warmth,
with simple love made bright.

Oh may we, like the shepherds, kneel
to look upon his face,
to feel the warmth and see the light
which filled that humble place.
Where Jesus is, no house is cold,
no shack too poor, to be
the very place where love shines out,
and peace will always be.

Today, there are several different kinds of carols.

THE LULLABY

such as:
Little Jesus, sweetly sleep, do not stir
and
Away in a manger, no crib for a bed

LIVELY DANCING SONGS

such as:
Ding dong! merrily on high
and
God rest you merry, gentlemen

THE CAROL HYMN

such as:
O little town of Bethlehem
and
While shepherds watched their flocks by night

THE NON-RELIGIOUS CAROL

such as:
The twelve days of Christmas
and
Good King Wenceslas

There is surprisingly little music written specially for Christmas, apart from carols. Two of the best-known works are oratorios. An oratorio is a kind of musical, usually religious, without actions, costumes or scenery. One of these well-known pieces is *Messiah* by Handel; the other is the *Christmas Oratorio* by J.S. Bach.

A composer named Corelli wrote a concerto *Made for Christmas Night*, and Vivaldi wrote one marked *For the most holy Nativity*. Alessandro Scarlatti wrote a Christmas cantata, which was a sort of mini-oratorio, and then, much later, Vaughan Williams composed a Christmas fantasia; and a Christmas opera, called *Amahl and the Night Visitors* was written by a man called Gian Carlo Menotti. You may have seen this on television.

A well-known British composer, Sir Benjamin Britten, took words from very old medieval songs and, keeping them in their old English form, set them to harp music. He wrote them for choir boy voices, and called the collection *A Ceremony of Carols*.

Handel's MESSIAH

Handel then wrote some music that could be played as the King's royal barge sailed down the River Thames. He called it the 'Water Music'. King George thought it was marvellous!

Handel, that was great music!

I will write more operas. People seem to like them too.

Handel went on to write grand operas for the next 30 years. Suddenly that style of music went out of fashion.

Perhaps I could write religious music now!

Handel began to write oratorios

I've written one about Esther, then one about Saul, then about the Israel-ites in Egypt

Now—what else?

In only 23 days, Handel wrote a new oratorio called 'The Messiah'

As the great Hallelujah Chorus of 'The Messiah' was sung, the King rose. He thought it was inspiring and absolutely wonderful!

It was the most popular music Handel had ever written. Today it is his best-known and best-loved work. People still stand up when the Hallelujah Chorus is sung!

Of 'The Messiah', Handel said:

I did think I did see all heaven before me, and the great God himself!

THE CHRISTINGLE SERVICE

Over two hundred years ago a lovely custom was begun in Germany. It was specially for the children of the Moravian Church in Marienborn. The Moravian Church was first formed in a part of Czechoslovakia called Moravia in the 15th century. Later, a group of Moravians emigrated to Saxony in Germany, and started new churches there.

John de Watteville, the man who led the first Christingle service, wanted to show the children in his church how the birth of Jesus could be like the beginning of a tiny flame within each one of them. This flame, he said, would be kept burning by their joy in knowing and loving Jesus Christ.

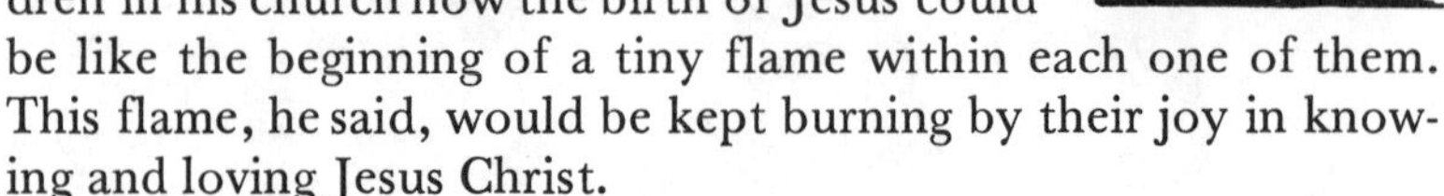

To make his words have more meaning, he gave each of the children a lighted candle, tied with a red ribbon. They carried the candles out of the church and into their homes, happy to have a reminder of the flame that was within their hearts.

Today, on Christmas Eve, the people of the Moravian Church still hold Christingle Services, and the children take home Christingle candles. Over the years the custom has developed so that now the candle is embedded in an orange, which represents the world. By the candle is a goose quill, split into several parts. These 'branches' stand for the spreading areas of the world over which Christ is the King. Onto the points of the quill are pushed raisins, nuts and sweets, to show that through God's goodness we receive food from the earth.

During the service, in which children take a very important part, the church is darkened and the candles the children hold are lit. As they are carried round the church, the candles give light, as the Christ-child did, to everyone there.

At the end of the service a Moravian carol is sung before the children go home with their Christingles.

Morning Star, O cheering sight,
Ere thou camst how dark earth's night.
Jesus mine,
In me shine,
Fill my heart with light divine.

Lots of other churches now copy the Moravian Christingle custom and hold similar services at Christmas time. Have you been to one? Was it exactly like the one described here? If your church does not know about Christingle services, why not suggest having one next year?

You could make simple Christingles by wrapping silver foil round the bottom of a small candle and pressing it into the top of an orange. Four cocktail sticks could take the place of the Moravian goose-quill. Spear these through nuts, raisins, or small sweets. Tie red ribbon round the orange.

PLAYS AND PANTOMIMES

In the Middle Ages very few people could read, so they had to be told stories from the Bible by the priests. The priests wanted the important stories of Christmas and Easter to be really well-known, so some of their church-goers acted them. The nave of the church was not filled with pews or chairs, as it is today, so there was plenty of room for acting the play.

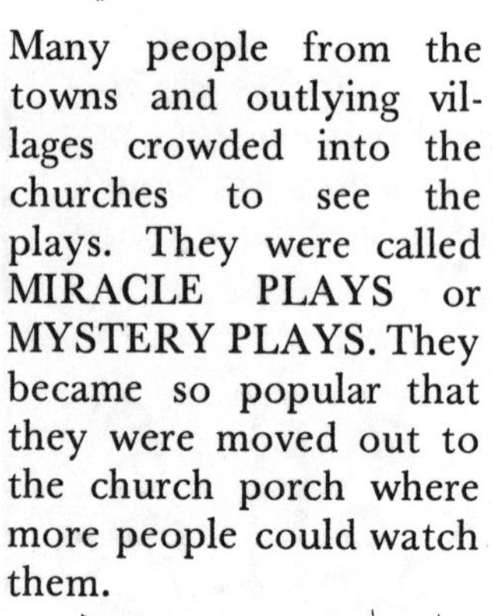

Many people from the towns and outlying villages crowded into the churches to see the plays. They were called MIRACLE PLAYS or MYSTERY PLAYS. They became so popular that they were moved out to the church porch where more people could watch them.

Later, the miracle plays were taken to the people in the market-places and streets of the towns. In order that the plays could be seen by the largest number of people, the stage had to be high, and able to be moved from one place to another. So carts on wheels were used for the players to act on, and these were pulled from place to place by horses, oxen, or even strong men. The stages were known as pageant carts.

When the play was performed outside, the performers added comedy, which was thought to be unsuitable inside a church.

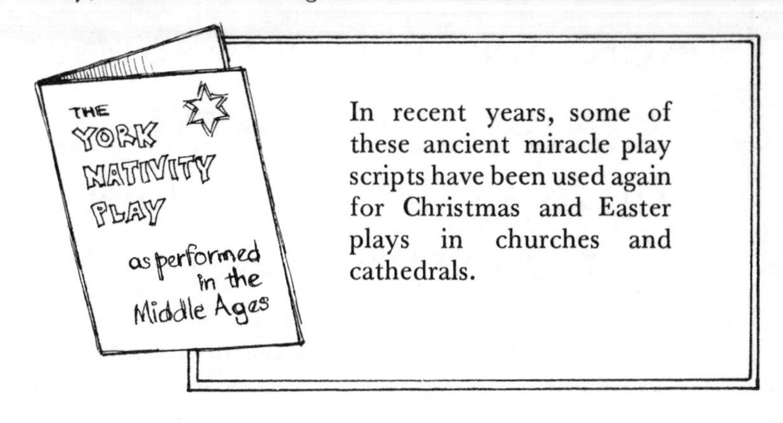

In recent years, some of these ancient miracle play scripts have been used again for Christmas and Easter plays in churches and cathedrals.

In the eighteenth century another custom began in France. Dancers who could also make people laugh gave special Christmas performances. Similar entertainments were soon being given in England, and, as a break from continual dancing, fairy stories were introduced.

Over the years these Christmas shows became far more elaborate.

Singers, acrobatic and juggling groups were asked to perform, also conjurors and ventriloquists. Pantomimes had come to stay.

PANTOMIME PUZZLE

Can you say what these pantomime titles are?

Answers on page 128

THE CHRISTMAS CRIB

Legend tells us that St Francis of Assisi was the first person to make a crib – a scene of the nativity. After he had visited Palestine and seen the cave of the nativity there, he went back to the Italian village of Greccio determined to make the Christmas story more real to the people there.

What do they really know, he thought, about living in a stable? So St Francis arranged a Christmas service in a cave on the hillside outside the village. He made it look like a stable, with live animals – an ass and an ox – tethered nearby.

Some stories tell us that he also had some of the villagers dressed as Mary and Joseph. St Francis preached to the people, there beside the manger, where they could see the conditions of the nativity.

Years later, the king of Naples, in Italy, made figures for a Christmas crib himself, and the queen and court ladies dressed them. In other years, he paid famous artists and sculptors to fashion wonderful new figures.

After that, everyone began to make cribs, or creches, and whole villages were employed to construct them.

Today, craftsmen in many European villages spend the whole year making crib figures which are sold all over the world. In Spain, where the earth is a rich red colour, the figures are made of terracotta, and in Germany the scenes are made almost entirely of wood from the vast forests there.

In Oberammergau, where a famous Easter play, or Passion play, is held every ten years, creche-making is an important town craft. In the wood-carving school there, children can go at the age of 14 to begin to learn the skills of creche-making.

Some creches today are very large, filled with life-size figures, and are erected out of doors. There is usually one in the centre of London, and people from all over the country visit it. Some cribs are in very strange places indeed, or made to look very strange. There is a permanent one underwater in Amalfi, in Italy, where life-size figures have been placed in the form of a nativity scene on the sea bed. At a special exhibition of cribs in France in 1966, a 'space creche' was set up. The nativity scene was set on a distant planet, and the three wise men were shown alighting from a jet!

Not all cribs need to be expensive or fantastically fashioned, though. Some of the simplest ones have given people the most pleasure, just as the one made by St Francis over seven hundred years ago.

The next few pages contain ideas for making a crib for your own home or church. It is designed so that you can use everyday objects, and is quite simple to make.

Follow these instructions to make a basic Eastern figure. You can adapt it for Mary, Joseph, a shepherd, or a wise man, by dressing it differently.

For each figure you will need:

a plastic teaspoon
a plastic cup or carton
scraps of material
felt tip pens
elastic bands
cotton wool

The shape itself is very simple to make, but you may need an adult's help to cut the cup.

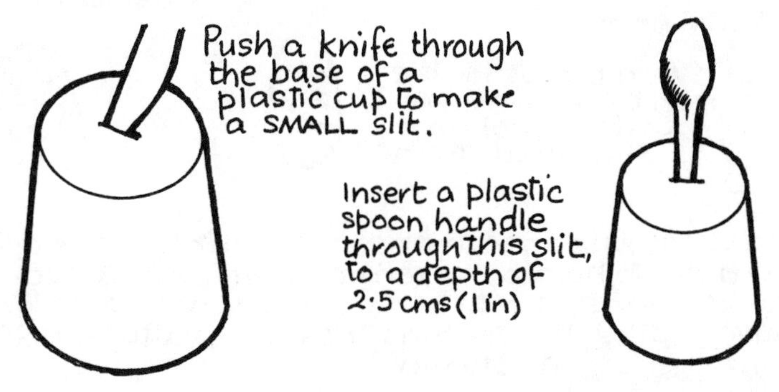

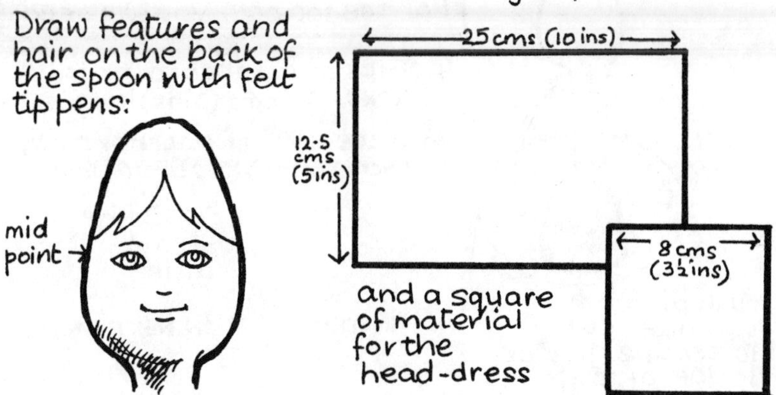

Wind the larger piece of material round as shown, and fasten with an elastic band round the neck:

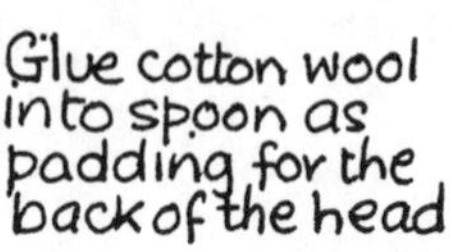

Glue cotton wool into spoon as padding for the back of the head

Fasten the small square of material on the head with an elastic band

For Mary, pin the material under her chin

Add beards for the men by glueing on cotton wool or shredded string

Dress the wise men in bright materials. Make gifts for them to hold by covering small objects, such as corks, beads, or plasticine shapes, with gold or silver foil. After dressing the figures, attach gifts as shown.

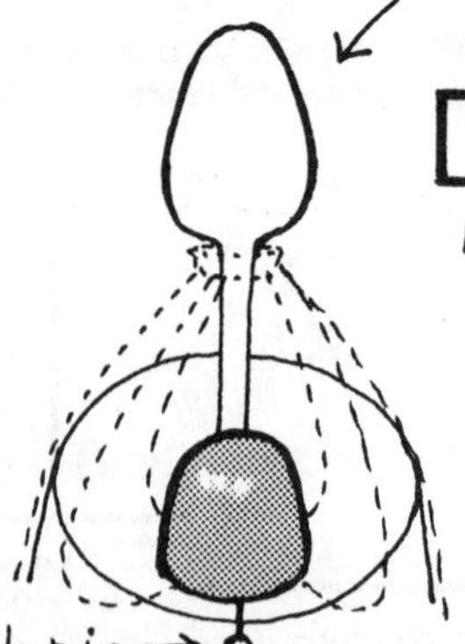

For the manger you will need:

4 strips of cardboard, or lolly sticks – 7·5cms (3ins) long.

A piece of stiff paper or card, 7·5cms (3ins) x 10cms (4 ins).

Plasticine
Straw
glue

INSTRUCTIONS ON NEXT PAGE

Glue the cardboard strips together to form two cross supports. Make plasticine feet for them to stand on.

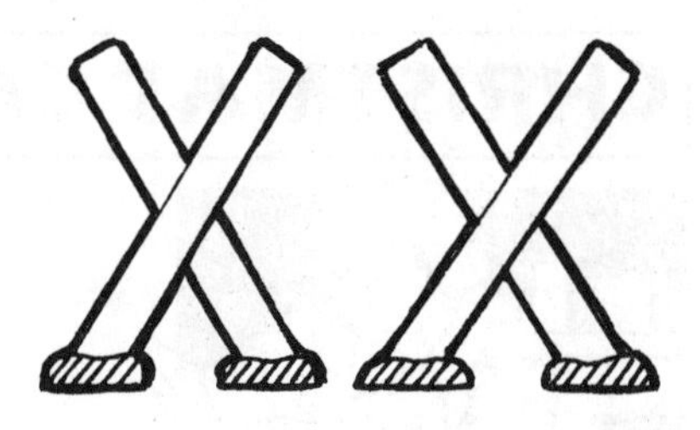

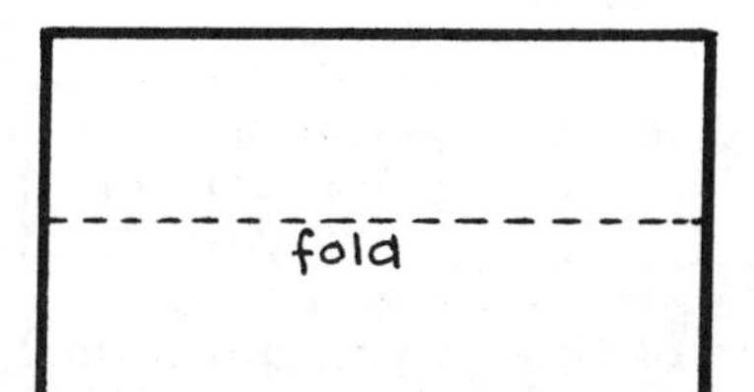

Fold the paper or card in half and lay between the cross supports.

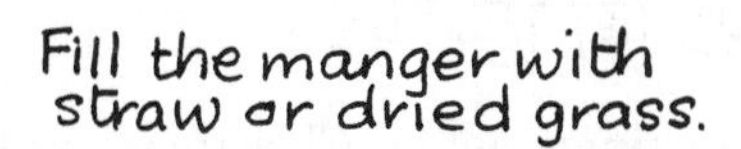

Fill the manger with straw or dried grass.

To make the baby:

Ask someone to help you to cut, or break, a plastic teaspoon so that is only 7·5cms (3ins) long. Pad the length of the back with cotton wool, and wind strips of white material round the whole baby, to look like swaddling clothes. Add features to face.

To make the stable:

Turn a cardboard carton on its side and cover the 'floor' with straw.

Arrange your figures round the manger inside.
(see page 70)

CHRISTMAS CARDS

Christmas is a time for remembering old friends and distant relatives, so we send our greetings in Christmas cards.

We like to receive cards ourselves, and use them to decorate the house.

Most of them are thrown away at the end of Christmas, but there are lots of things you could do with them. (See pages 112-113)

In Victorian times, when Christmas cards were novel, they were really treasured.

Oh what a lovely picture – so sweet! I must keep it always!

Look out for precious Victorian albums filled with Christmas cards; they can sometimes be found in antique shops.

Less than 150 years ago the very first Christmas card in Britain was delivered. As far as we know, the first one was designed by John Horsley at the request of his friend, Henry Cole. It looked something like the picture on the opposite page.

Notice the wealthy family enjoying a Christmas party. The smaller panels, though, show that poorer people were remembered, too.

You could make your own Christmas card based on this very first design:

Trace, or copy, the thick outlines onto a piece of white card. Draw pictures of your own family in the middle section. The side panels could hold pictures of your pets, your house and garden, or of any hobbies or interests your family have. Colour the card, and write your own Christmas message under the main design.

Before Mr Cole and Mr Horsley, in about 1843, popularised the sending of Christmas cards, children were encouraged by their teachers to write Christmas pieces for their parents. One or two sentences, carrying Christmas greetings, were beautifully handwritten for them. (This also showed how the child's handwriting was progressing!)

Dearest Mama and Papa, I wish you both the compliments of this joyful season,
Your affectionate son, Arthur.

In the early days, the designs on Christmas cards were often irrelevant to the birth of Jesus in Bethlehem. The cards were made as pretty and as decorative as possible, and the Victorians used to make many by hand, using lace, ribbon, and patterned paper.

Design a card for a very dear relative or friend, using lace, paper doyleys, flower pictures, and ribbon.

Perhaps, if you sent one made in this way, it would be treasured by someone for many years.

Robins have always been popular Christmas card birds. Look at these two – one from a very early card, and one from a modern card.

Trace or copy these robins for your own cards and decorations.

Here are some suggestions for making your own Christmas cards, based on some of the earliest cards produced.

Tab Card

You will need:
a piece of paper or card 20cms x 12.5cms (or 8ins x 5ins), another piece 4cms x 5cms (or 1½ins x 2ins), felt tip pens, glue, and a clean iced lolly stick.

Fold the larger piece of paper or card to make a card shape.

Trace the stable outline onto the centre of the card, with the bottom line above the mid-line of the card (see diagram). Cut out on the thick lines.

Re-fold the card and draw a picture of Mary and the baby on the inside sheet of the card, within the 'window' you have made. (You could copy or trace the drawing from the next page.)

Colour the picture, and also the shape of the stable on the front of the card.

STABLE OUTLINE

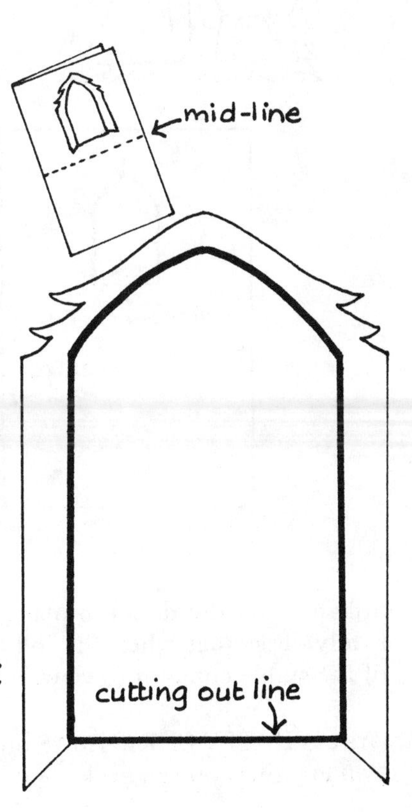

On the small piece of paper draw and colour the stable doors (see below). Trim the lolly stick to about 9cms (or 3½ins) and attach it to the back of the small card.

Now open out your large card, and lay the smaller one (doors facing you) so that it hides the nativity picture.

Glue all round this, as shown, being careful not to get the glue too near the doors or the lolly stick.

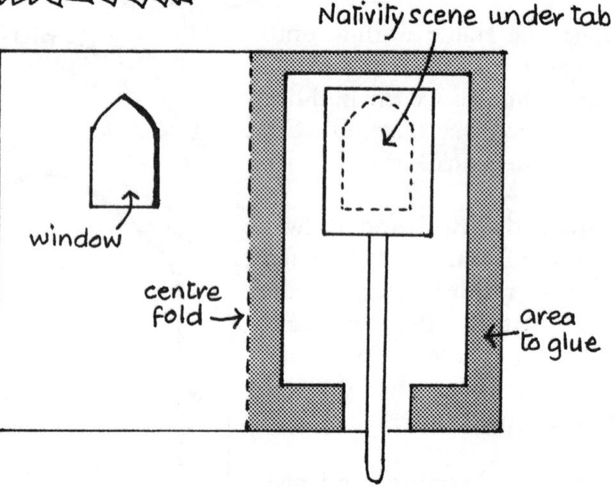

Still holding the doors in place, close the card so that it sticks firmly. Test that when the lolly stick is pulled down the inside of the stable comes into view.

Write A HAPPY CHRISTMAS on the front of the card, and your own greetings on the back.

An open-the-door card

You will need a piece of card or thick paper 24cms x 10cms (or 9ins x 3½ins). Measure the card into three equal sections.

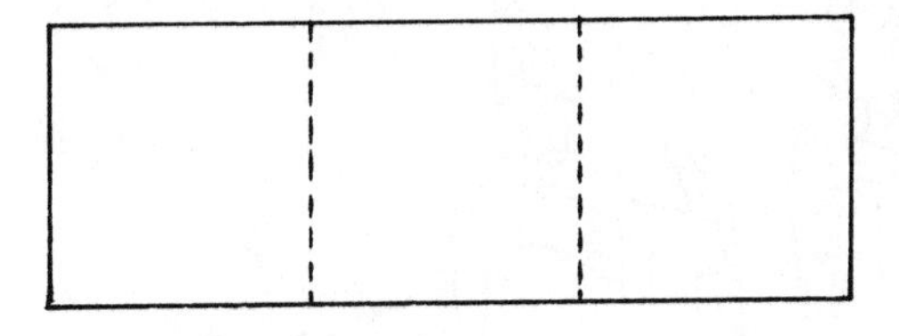

Now fold it like this

first fold

second fold

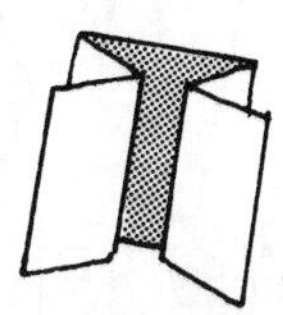

Open out the card. On the centre of the card draw and colour a picture of the nativity inside the stable, and add the shepherds and the wise men at either side.

Your card should look something like this:

Make the outside folds look like wooden stable doors. Fold the card so that the inside pictures are hidden until the doors are pulled aside.

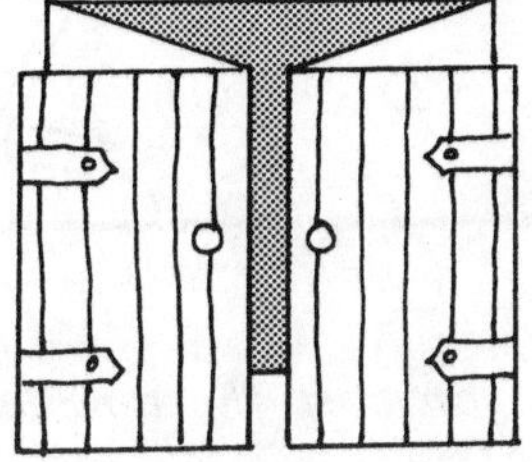

Here are two pictures to trace on to other cards you could make. Colour them brightly.

Use some of the templates on pages 125-126 to make other Christmas cards to your own design.

DISPLAYING THE CHRISTMAS CARDS

We all like to make the Christmas cards we receive into part of our Christmas decorations. There are several ways of doing this.

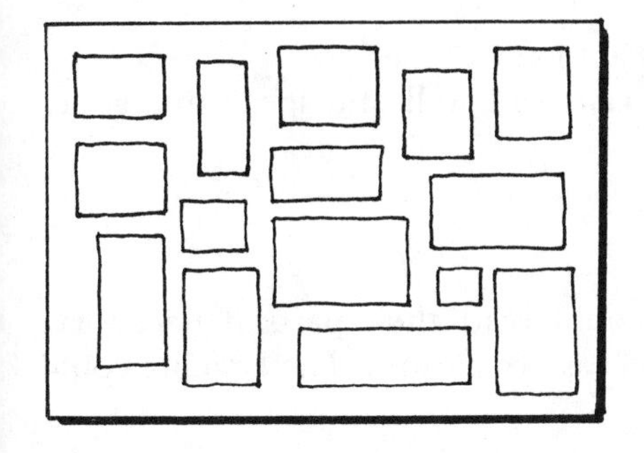

With stamp hinges, glue or sticky tape, attach the cards in a display on large sheets of coloured paper. You can then pin these sheets on to a wall, or press them to a wall using small balls of blu-tack.

If you do not want your cards to fall open while on display, seal them with a small piece of sticky tape to keep them closed. This can be cut through quite cleanly afterwards.

Peg the cards to strips of crepe paper or ribbon . . .

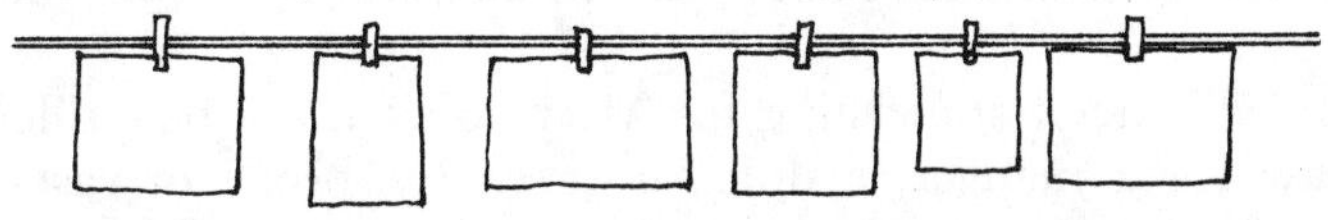

. . . or push them into flat strips of plasticine so that they will stand firmly on a flat surface. In between each card you could put ivy leaves or silver balls.

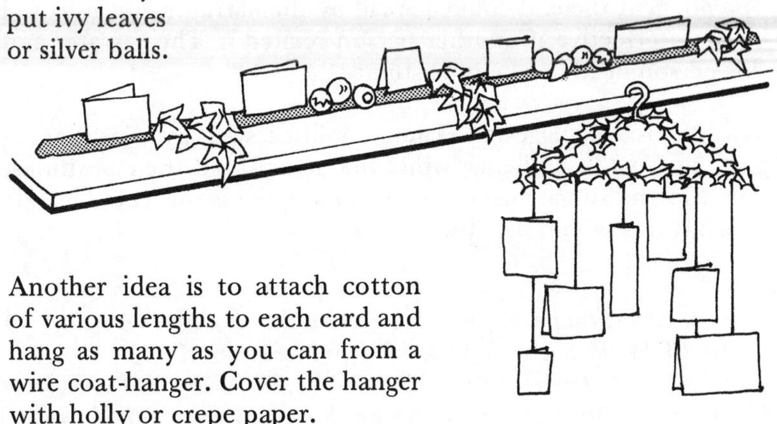

Another idea is to attach cotton of various lengths to each card and hang as many as you can from a wire coat-hanger. Cover the hanger with holly or crepe paper.

A NATIVITY PLAY

This nativity play, which you could act with a group of friends, is fairly straightforward, but a little different from usual.

You will need the following actors:
A narrator: someone who can read well and speak in a good, clear voice
Balak, king of Moab
Balaam, a prophet of Israel
An Israelite

These three characters could read their parts if necessary. They should be dressed in eastern clothes. The Israelite could read from a scroll.

Mary
Joseph
Shepherds – three or more
Wise men – three or more

Mary has only one sentence to say, but she should have a carrying voice, as she has to speak while she is still unseen. One of the wise men has to speak before he enters, and they have one sentence each to say while kneeling before the baby.

You will need something for Mary to sit on, a box filled with straw for a manger, a doll for the baby, boxes or vases to represent the wise men's gifts.

The poem at the end could be read by the narrator, but it would be more effective if another person recited it. The narrator and this person need not be in costume.

Two carols are suggested. These could be sung by those taking part, or by the audience while the actors hold their positions. If music and singing cannot be included, the carols could be left out, but this would be a pity.

The conversation between Balak and Balaam is based on Numbers 24.10-13,17. Isaiah's prophecy is from Isaiah 60.2,6.

Ideas on how to dress the actors are given on pages 86-87.

Set the scene for your nativity play like this:

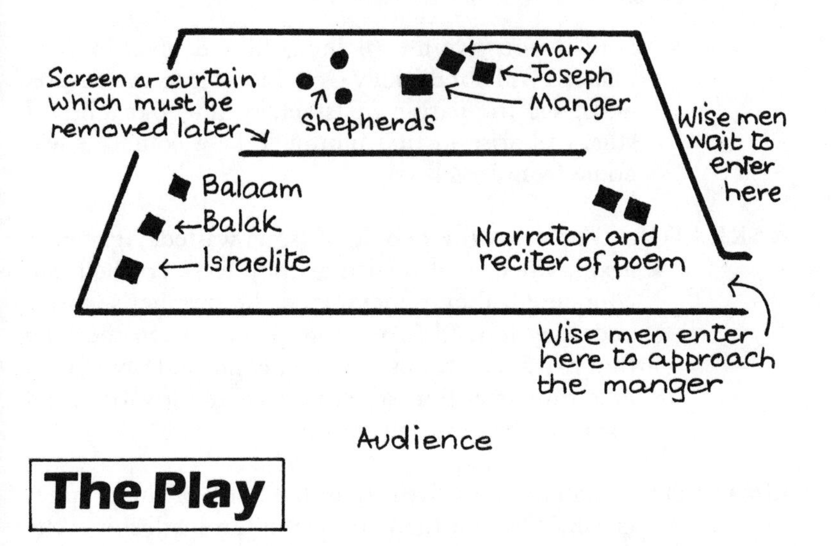

The Play

All performers should be in position, with stage hands ready to draw the curtain or remove the screen that will reveal the stable scene.

NARRATOR: A long, long time before Jesus was born, the Hebrew people looked forward to the time when they would be able to live in their own land. They believed that God had promised it to them. 'We shall be a great nation,' they said to each other.
Some of them remembered a man called Balaam speaking with the king of an enemy tribe.

BALAK: I am King Balak of Moab. I hate the Israelite people. I order you, Balaam, to put a curse on them!

BALAAM: I cannot do any such thing! God is with them, and will protect them.

BALAK *(Angrily)*: Three times I have asked you to curse them. Three times you have refused. Instead, all you will do is to bless them, and tell me they are loved of God!

BALAAM: Even if you give me all the gold and silver in your palace I will not disobey God. I look into the future, and I see the nation of Israel. A king, like a bright star, will arise in that nation. Like a comet he will come from Israel!

NARRATOR: For years the people of Israel waited. Again and again, when it seemed that they were crushed and conquered, they remembered the prophet's words, and they looked forward to a time when the king that had been promised would come and save them. And time after time other men came forward to tell them to keep waiting for him.

ISRAELITE *(Reading)*: It is written in the book of the prophet Isaiah, 'On you the light of the Lord will shine; the brightness of his presence will be with you . . . Great caravans of camels will come, from Midian and Ephah. They will come from Sheba, bringing gold and incense. People will tell the good news of what the Lord has done!'

NARRATOR: 'But where is this king?' the people asked when they were in trouble. 'When will he come?'

ISRAELITE: We expected him to come in glory, a conquering man, ready to lead us into battle!

MARY, *from behind screen*: But he came to me, a young girl living in a country village.

The screen or curtain is removed to show the audience the scene in the stable. The SHEPHERDS should be kneeling in position, and all remain still while the carol is sung.

Carol: A child this day is born (verses 1,2,4,7), or Away in a manger.

During the last verse, the shepherds get up and depart.

WISE MAN, *off stage*: Where is the baby born to be king of the Jews? We saw a bright star when it came up in the east, and we have come to worship him.

The WISE MEN enter as the NARRATOR speaks.

NARRATOR: Travelling with great caravans of camels they will come, bringing gold and incense. The wise men have come to learn the good news of God's gift to the people of Israel.

The WISE MEN kneel and offer their gifts.

1st WISE MAN: I bring you gold, fit for a king.

2nd WISE MAN: I bring you frankincense, fit for God himself.

3rd WISE MAN: I bring you myrrh, fit for a man of the people.

NARRATOR (or other person):

No fanfare told his coming,
no palace gave him space;
only a few knew who he was
and gazed into his face,
knowing that he, who lay in straw
beside his mother's knee,
was God's great promise come to earth
to make the people free.

Carol: Christmas Day is far away (Sing New Songs, 23) or As with gladness men of old.

The actors leave the stage, those in the actual stable scene last of all.

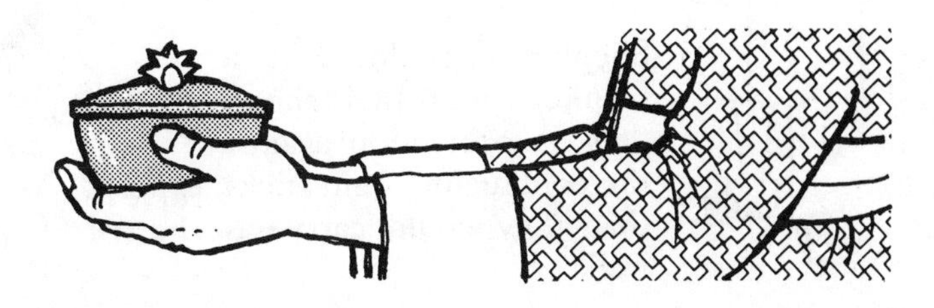

DRESSING THE NATIVITY PLAY

Here are some suggestions for making simple eastern costumes for your play.

MARY

She will need a long dress – perhaps you could use a plain nightdress – and a head-dress. Make this from a large cotton scarf, an old curtain, or a piece of sheet. Wrap it as shown.

Mary is usually shown in pictures wearing blue and white, so keep to those colours if possible.

JOSEPH, SHEPHERDS, INNKEEPER

A very simple cloak made from a dressing-gown tied round the waist would do. To make the men look eastern, put a fairly large white scarf or piece of sheeting on the head and fasten with a cord or plaited wool.

Shepherds could wear a blanket round their shoulders as protection against the cold nights. Find sticks that they could carry, as well.

WISE MEN

These need to be dressed with as much colour and richness as possible, so that they contrast well with the poorer people.

Use scarves with gold threads, flowing coloured robes, gold shoes, ear-rings and elaborate head-dresses.

The paper hat shown on page 101 would be an excellent choice for a wise man. Make it with strong foil in silver or red.

Make the wise men's gifts by covering a few everyday objects with paper or material.

Cover a sweet tin, or small biscuit tin, with gold paper. Spray a fir-cone gold. Fix it to the lid with sellotape or blu-tack.

Cover an empty king-size yoghurt pot with silver foil or a rich-looking material. Make the top by covering a conker or acorn or marble with foil, and twist as shown.

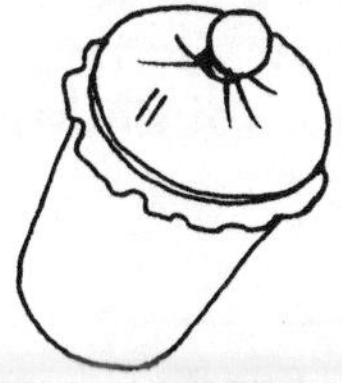

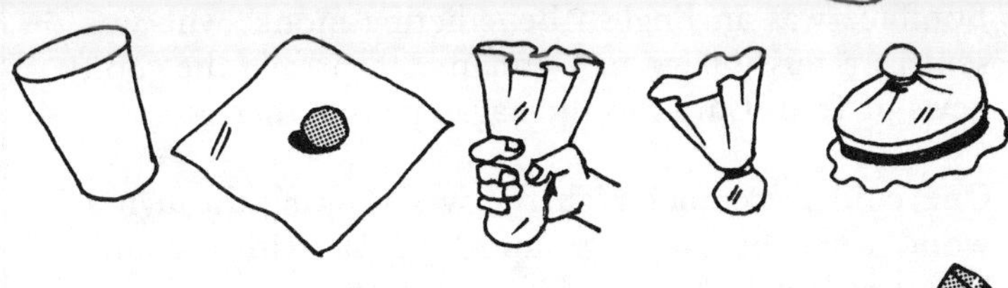

Spread open the foil and fix on the top of the pot with ribbon or sellotape.

You could use a vase for the last present. Cover it or use it as it is.

CHRISTMAS TREES

There are stories of trees, and tree branches, being brought indoors long before Christian times. The Roman festival of Saturnalia, in mid-winter, was celebrated to honour Saturn, the god of all growing things. At that time, branches of evergreen trees were carried indoors and hung with trinkets.

The Celtic Druids also decorated branches of trees, hanging them with gilt apples, in honour of their own particular gods.

These winter customs, where the world of nature was brought indoors, were continued by Christians when they came together to celebrate Christmas.

There is an old story, or legend, which tells us how the fir tree became a very special symbol of Christmas.

Boniface was an English Benedictine monk, who was sent as a missionary to Germany, to preach the good news of Jesus Christ to the pagan people there.

One cold December night he was walking through a wood when he saw a group of people with a young boy tied ready to be sacrificed under a sacred oak tree.

Boniface was horrified, and rushed into the pagan meeting-place. Rescuing the boy, he took an axe and began to chop down the oak tree.

The people looked on, stunned, as the brave man risked their fury and felled the sacred oak.

As the tree crashed down, Boniface noticed, growing among its roots, a small fir tree.

'From now on,' Boniface told them, 'this fir tree will be a holy emblem. It is a sign of peace, for we build our homes with its wood; it is a sign of life eternal, for its leaves are always green; and, because it points to heaven, it will be a symbol of the Christ-child who pointed us to God.'

There are many other fascinating stories about the little fir tree that became our Christmas tree. One says that Martin Luther, a great German preacher, was the first person to decorate one with lights. One Christmas Eve, seeing the stars shining through the fir trees outside his home, he had an idea. He took a tree indoors for his children and hung candles on it: they reminded him of the shining stars. That was in 1530, and the tradition of decorating young fir trees for homes had begun in Germany.

Three hundred years later a German prince, Albert, came to Britain to marry the British queen – our Queen Victoria. When they had children, Albert remembered his own childhood Christmases, and the Christmas trees that were always brought in to be decorated. 'Let's have one here at Windsor Castle,' he said, and so in 1841 the first Christmas tree came to Britain for Queen Victoria and Prince Albert's children.

Many people copied the royal family's idea, and cut down young fir trees to take into their houses. At first these were simply decorated with fruit, almonds and sweets, and were only for the children of the family.

Now, nearly every family in Britain has a Christmas tree at Christmas time. Some are real trees, cut from specially grown plantations. Others are artificial, and can be used year after year. Christmas trees are set up in town squares and market places, and there are trees in churches, schools, hospitals and even prisons.

THE WINTER FLAME

East winds, cold rain, and little sun,
  No leaves, few flowers, fruit gone:
Winter, with dark and dismal days,
  Winter has come.

But into winter Christmas comes
  Like some bright, flaming fire,
With warmth and crackle and colour and light,
  To lift us higher.

What is the flame that first began
  To kindle this fire of joy?
What would the winter be like, without
  A baby boy?

All our excitement at Christmas,
  This warmth in the winter cold,
Began in a stable in Bethlehem,
  So we are told.

Over the years we look back and see
  How shepherds and wise men came;
In the middle of winter we worship him too,
  Exactly the same.

CHRISTMAS MORNING

Lying awake in the dark,
wide awake, eyes awake,
   is it morning?
The whole house sleeps,
dark and silent and still;
but it feels like a wide-awake morning,
   holiday time, leaping up time,
when the light pulls me awake
to the fun of a no-school day.
   Is it morning?
My eyes search the dark:
my ears ought to hear
the extraordinary sounds of an extraordinary day.
It IS special today –
   doesn't anyone know? Why do they sleep?
   How can they dream? But they do.
I'll explore in the dark,
feel round in the dark,
for surprises I think should be there:
   a long stocking-shape,
   with a bump and a lump,
   with a softness and smoothness,
   and a mandarin toe.
My stocking – yes, hanging
heavy and awkward,
where it last night lay limp and forlorn.
   I feel jumpy and spiky,
   yet happy and warm.
It makes me remember last year's December:
at first it was painfully slow,
but then so exciting,
   the Christmas tree lighting,
   the postman, the cards,
   and the sound of the carols,
   the cold and the promise of snow.
Thank you, oh thank you, little Lord Jesus,
for coming each year and filling me so
   with this lovely warm glow.

JUST ONCE

Held fast by loving arms,
  Warm, wanted, loved, secure,
Dreaming his baby dreams
  Behind that stable door:

Just once, and only once,
  Into the world he came.
His parents had no noble rank,
  No wealth, no land, no fame.

Just once, and wonderingly,
  The shepherds knelt to see
The baby, Saviour of the world,
  Upon his mother's knee.

Just once, in grandeur fine,
  The wise men from afar
Discovered where the baby slept
  By following a star.

Just once, and far away;
  But, though the world is torn,
Divided, yet each year he comes,
  Each year he is re-born.

At home, in church, in school,
  Each year, and evermore,
We celebrate his one-time birth,
  And see that stable door.

EVERGREENS AT CHRISTMAS

It seems strange to think that a hundred years ago the only Christmas decorations that people had in their homes at Christmas time, apart from a Christmas tree, were branches of holly, laurel or fir, or trails of ivy. Leaves of the bay tree and the rosemary bush were also brought indoors to give a lovely herbal scent. Today we have many decorations to choose from, made of coloured paper, plastic, gold and silver foil, and glass.

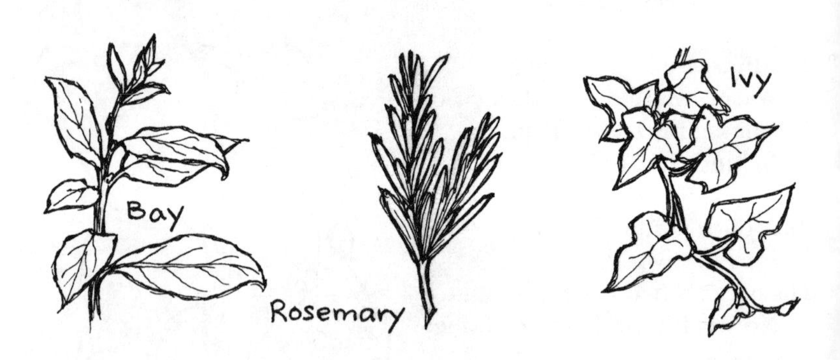

Evergreens had been popular for a long time as Christmas decorations, but it was thought to be a bad omen to bring them into the house before Christmas Eve, or to leave them up after January 6. Nowadays we decorate much earlier in readiness for Christmas, but most places are bare again by January 6.

Although many people feel that Christmas is not complete without a sprig of mistletoe in their homes, it is very rarely seen decorating churches. Mistletoe has always seemed to be a plant holding magical properties. It has no roots in the ground, but lives hanging in circular masses high up in other trees. Once, too, it was associated with pagan religions. It was a plant sacred to the Druids and to people of Scandinavian countries, the Norsemen. It has never quite lost its pagan associations. There are stories of a mistletoe branch being made into a small but deadly weapon with which Balder, the sun god, was slain.

Mistletoe was supposed to be a 'truce' plant: where it hung, enemies were ordered to stop fighting. Some ancient people thought that by displaying it during a thunderstorm it would give their house protection from lightning and fire.

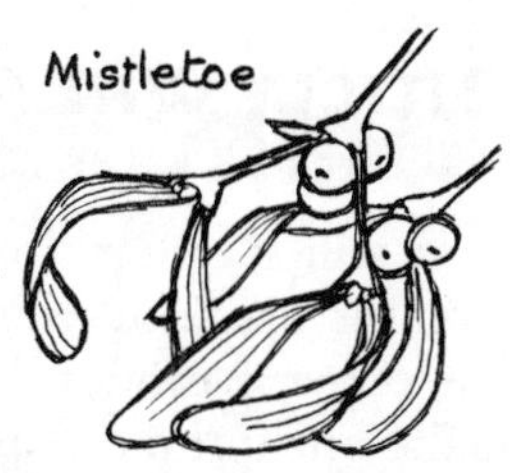

Now, when we hang it in our homes, it has become a symbol of love, with a tradition of kissing under it.

Before Christmas trees became popular, people used to hang a circle of greenery in their homes. It was decorated with apples, paper flowers and candles. Under it most of the Christmas activities took place – carols were sung, food eaten, and games played. Sometimes from the centre a piece of mistletoe would be hung, and the whole decorated ring was then known as 'the kissing bough'.

There is a story of a miraculous hawthorn tree that blooms at Christmas time instead of at the usual time in the spring. The Bible records that when Jesus was killed, a man called Joseph of Arimathaea, a secret follower of Jesus, asked Pilate if he could take Jesus' body and bury it.

Later, a legend grew that Joseph travelled to Britain and visited Glastonbury. There he stuck the thorn stick he carried into the ground. It took root, and bloomed in time for Christmas. Every year after that, at Christmas time, people came from far away to look at the hawthorn tree in full flower. Although the tree itself was later cut down by orders of the Puritans, cuttings from its branches were planted, and some still grow to-day.

HOLLY WREATH

You will see that the front doors of some houses are hung with wreaths made of evergreens at this time of year. Some wreaths are expensive ones, bought from florists' shops, but you could make one quite cheaply yourself.

You will need:

- a length of thick wire, or a metal coat hanger
- evergreens such as holly, laurel or fir
- red ribbon, and a few red decorations
- cotton to tie
- gold spray and glitter, if possible, but they are not essential

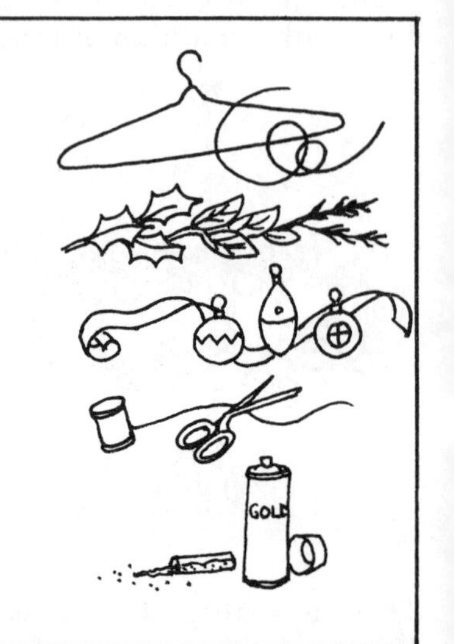

Pull the coat hanger into a circle, or bend and fasten the wire to make a ring.

Tie twigs of evergreens all round the wire to cover it. If you are using gold spray, put it on now, lightly touching the leaves with it. Sprinkle on glitter while the paint is still wet. Add decorations at intervals between the leaves, and tie the ribbon in a bow. Attach it to the top.

HOLLY BALL

Ask if you may have a large potato for this decoration. You will also need sprigs of holly, and some trails of ivy, if possible. And a length of thin string, a large needle or a skewer, and some red ribbon.

Thread the string through the centre of the potato, using the needle. If you do not have a needle, ask a grown-up to push a skewer through the potato so that the string can be threaded through.

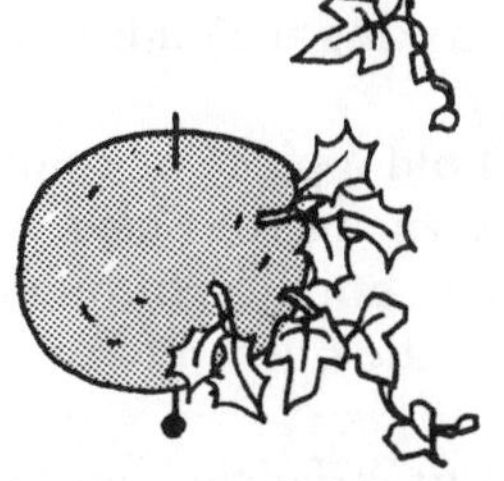

Tie a knot in the string at the base, and make a bow with the ribbon just above this knot. Stick sprigs of holly and ivy all over the potato to cover it.

DOOR TRAILS

If you have some ivy in the garden, make some decorative trails over the doors of your rooms.

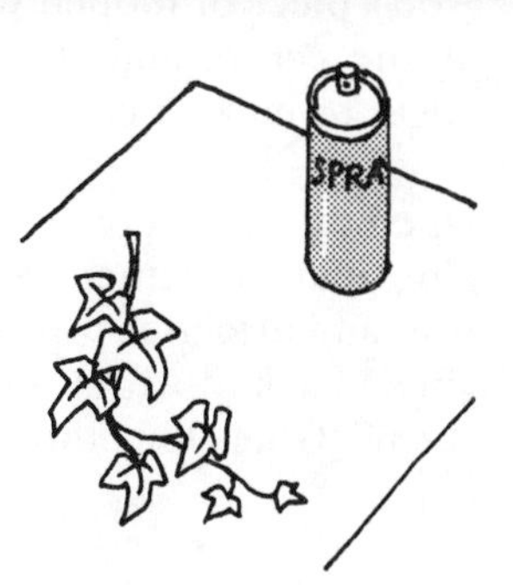

Lay the ivy on newspaper and spray the tips of the leaves with gold spray. Attach the ivy over the doorway, securing it with blu-tack or sellotape. Add a large red crepe paper bow in the centre.

DECORATIONS TO MAKE

Christmas decorations cost a lot to buy, but some can be made very cheaply if you have a little time, and patience.

LANTERN

You will need:
- a toilet roll centre,
- cooking foil,
- coloured paper,
- wool for hanging,
- glue, scissors, sellotape.

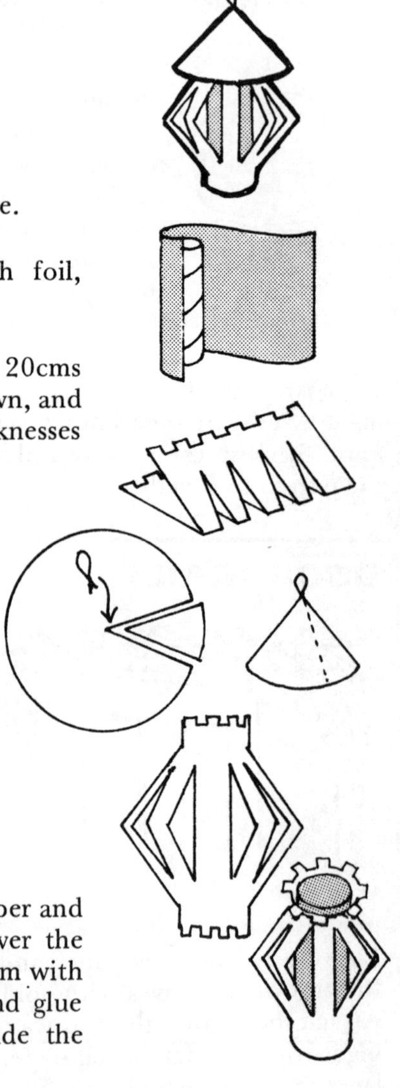

Cover the cardboard roll with foil, tucking the ends in neatly.

Fold a piece of coloured paper, 20cms x 15cms (or 8ins x 6ins) as shown, and cut notches through both thicknesses in the open side.

Cut triangles out of the folded side.

Draw round a tea plate on another piece of coloured paper, and cut out. Cut out a segment.

Add a piece of looped wool at the centre and glue cut edges to make a cone.

Open up the cut rectangle of paper and glue ends together. Slide it over the roll, and attach it top and bottom with glue. Tuck bottom tabs in and glue them. Glue the top tabs inside the cone.

HANGING WINDMILL

These Christmas tree decorations would look very bright and cheerful if you made them in silver foil, but you could make them in plain coloured paper instead.

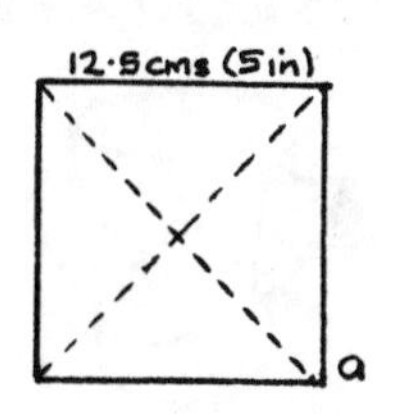

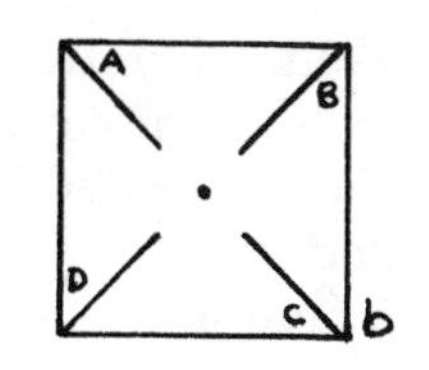

Fold a square of paper as shown (a). Cut on the folded lines to about 2cms (or ¾in) from the centre (b). Now bring the points A, B, C and D to the centre point and fix with a paper clip: one that opens out at the back (c).

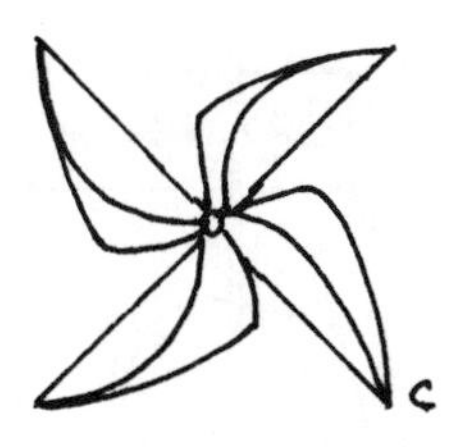

Attach a length of wool at one of the points, and hang it from the tree. If you made several larger ones they could hang from a central light, over the table.

SWEET BAG

Fold more paper to make these little bags. Fill them with sweets and hang them on the tree, or use them to hold small gifts for your friends.

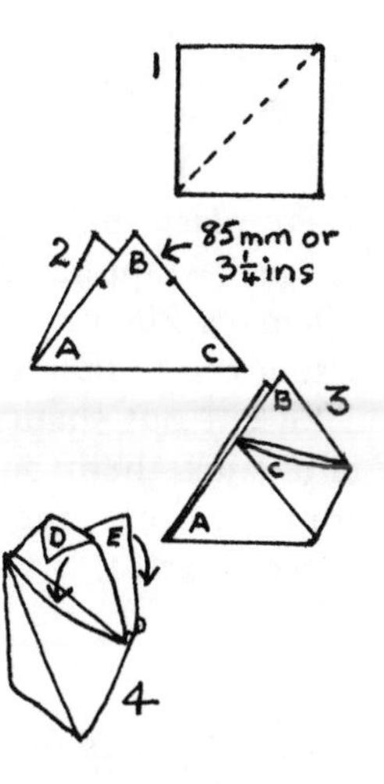

You need a piece of paper about 20cms (or 8ins) square. Fold it in half diagonally (1). Mark each side 85mm (or 3¼ins) from point B. Fold C to touch the mark between A and B. Turn it over and fold A to touch the mark between B and C. Open out slightly and tuck D and E into the 'pockets' on either side. This will give you a bag shape. Attach wool for hanging.

DECORATIONS FOR THE TABLE

These 'funny face' cups will add fun to your Christmas table. For each paper cup you will need paper ears. Trace the shape and cut out.

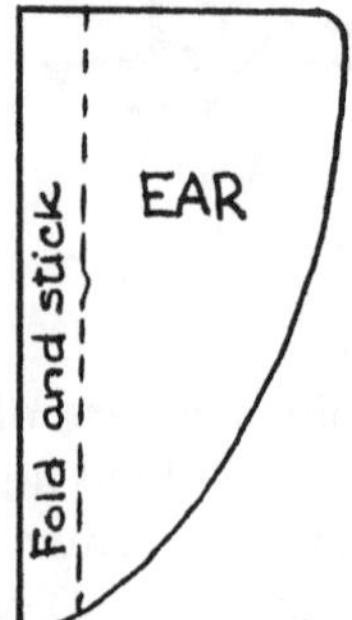

Fold on dotted lines and stick to the cup sides. Make the face by adding sequins and sticky paper, and draw a mouth.

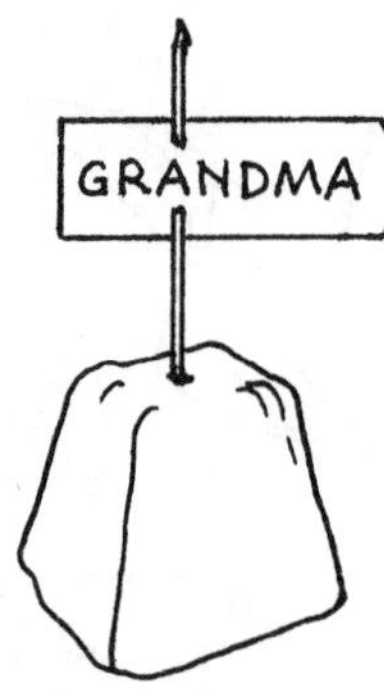

To show your family and friends where to sit, make these place name holders. For each one, cut out a segment of an egg box. Paint it or cover it with cooking foil. Write a name on a strip of paper and pierce it with a cocktail stick. Push the other end of the stick through the top of the egg carton segment.

Make place mats by cutting sheets of gay wrapping paper to about 30cms x 20cms (or 12ins x 8ins). Using the templates on pages 125-126, cut out shapes in plain paper and stick them on the mat. You could also cut out large letters to name the mat.

To label plates of sandwiches, use the holly leaf template (page 125) and cut the shape out of card. Write names of the sandwich fillings on the centre, and push a cocktail stick through each one.

PAPER HATS

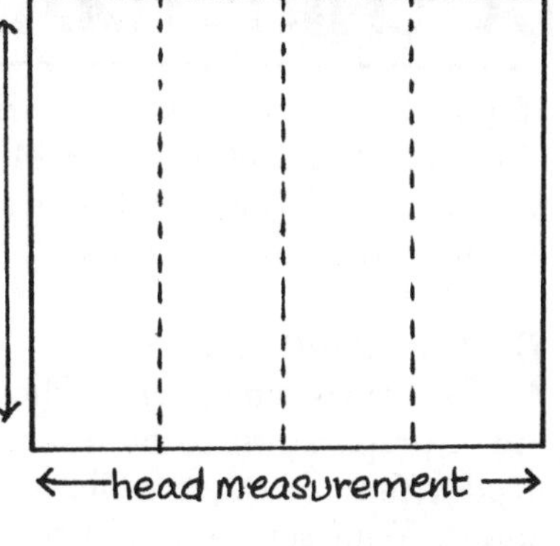

Make one for each member of the family!

From a packet of crepe paper, cut out a rectangle to the measurements shown here.

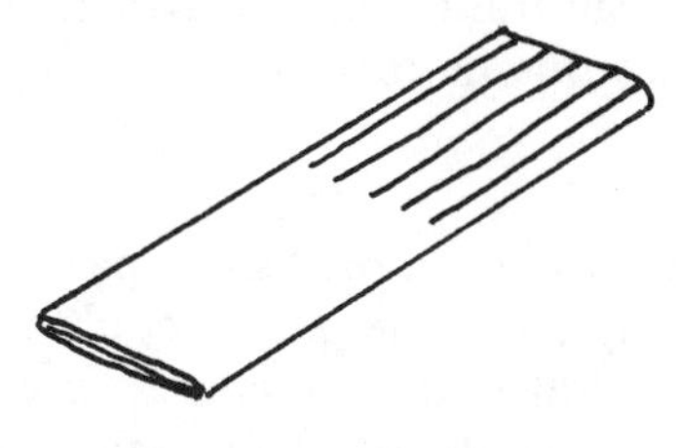

Fold in four. Cut through all layers to about half way.

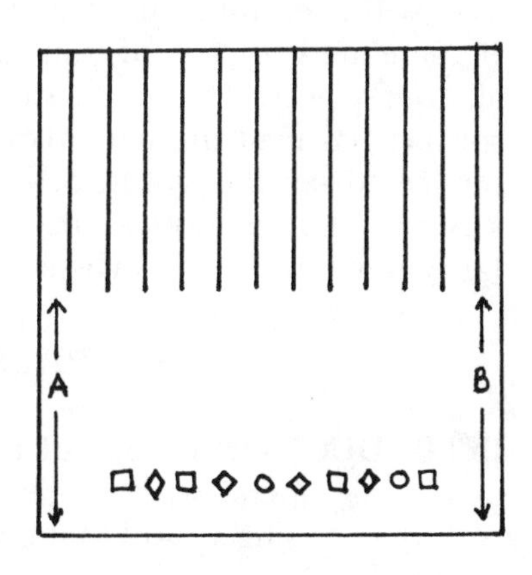

Open out and add scraps of contrasting paper along the bottom, in different shapes and sizes. Glue A to B.

Put your hand firmly round the cut strips and tie wool at the bottom of the cut ends.

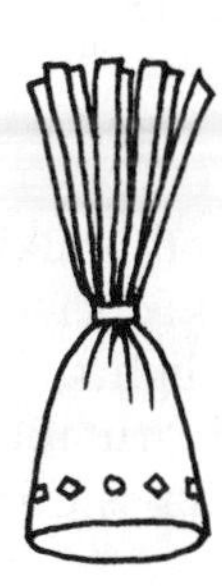

When the hat is worn these cut strips will fan out and hang down all round the hat.

If you do not have any crepe paper, try making the hats with sheets of Christmas wrapping paper.

Instead of the wool, you could tie a contrasting coloured ribbon to make a decorative bow for the front of the hat.

A CHRISTMAS SERVICE

If you have been asked to arrange a service for Christmas, in church or for a school assembly, you could discuss the following ideas with a group of friends, and decide how they could be adapted to suit your needs.

To think about together
At Christmas time, when there is so much excitement, and so much preparation to be done, men, women and children really need a time of quiet, when they can think what Christmas is all about. Your service could provide this moment of peace for all who join in it.
Preparation
You will need four 'speakers' who will each read short passages. If there are very few of you taking part, one person could take all four places. There is a short chorus that is said after each speaker has read the sentences. You could ask the people at the service to say the words, or just those who are conducting the service. Whoever says them, the words should be recited in a fairly low tone, and slowly, so that there is a feeling of peace.

THE SERVICE

INTRODUCTION by one of the speakers: Christmas is almost here, with all its excitement and gladness. Let us sing a carol that gives us this feeling of joy.

CAROL sung by all: Ding dong! merrily on high

1st SPEAKER: Hurrying, scurrying, swaying and talking; anxious to buy, eager to sell, the shopkeepers and customers move to and fro. Glaring lights, loud music, men and women pushing and grumbling, children pointing, and babies crying; this is Christmas.

CHORUS: And peace on earth.

2nd SPEAKER: Tired mothers, cooking and planning; impatient fathers, and excited children; presents hidden,

Christmas trees ready, balloons bursting, and bells ringing; this is Christmas.

CHORUS: And peace on earth.

3rd SPEAKER: Carols to learn, music to play; nativity plays, concerts, and end-of-term parties; making secret presents, hanging up decorations, colouring Christmas cards; ready for the holiday, for visitors and for visiting; this is Christmas.

CHORUS: And peace on earth.

4th SPEAKER *(Quietly and slowly)*: There were no celebrations that first Christmas. Just a sleepy town, an outhouse stable where the straw rustled and a lamp flickered. Just a mother and her baby; this was Christmas.

CHORUS: And peace on earth.

CAROL sung by all, very quietly: Away in a manger, *or* The Rocking Carol.

READING: The story of the shepherds, Luke 2.8-20, from a modern translation of the Bible.

4th SPEAKER: Let us pray.
We stand still, O God, in the middle of our Christmas planning. We are quiet, O God, in the middle of our Christmas noise. We are thinking of you, O God, in the stillness and quietness, and we remember your gift to the world. Help us to take time now, while we are so involved in all the Christmas excitement, to whisper, 'Peace on earth'. Amen

SANTA CLAUS

In nearly every country in the world there is a legend of someone who distributes gifts at Christmas time. In many European countries, and in America, this gift-bringer is known as Santa Claus, or Father Christmas.

Santa Claus is another name for St Nicholas, who was a real man, born about 270AD, the son of wealthy Christian parents. When he grew up he became the Bishop of Myra, a town in the country now called Turkey. He died about 340AD. Apart from these facts, little is really known about Nicholas, except that he had a very kind heart and loved giving to anyone in need.

The best-known story that is told about Nicholas is one of his generosity. A poor man and his three daughters lived in the same town as Nicholas. Each of the girls was beautiful, and each hoped to marry. But, in those days, the father of the bride had to provide a good sum of money as a marriage settlement, and this poor father could not do so.

Nicholas, hearing of the family's difficulties, went to their house one night and dropped a bag full of gold coins through a window. The poor man was delighted to find that suddenly he had enough money to pay his eldest daughter's dowry, and she was soon married.

A second time the same thing happened, and the second girl could get married. The father was very curious to know who was being so generous, and lay in wait to see if a third gift would be made for his youngest daughter.

When the bag of gold was dropped through the window, the poor man recognised the giver as Bishop Nicholas, and fell to his knees, thanking him. Nicholas, however, did not want anyone to know of his generosity, and begged the father to say nothing.

We can assume, though, that the poor man found it very difficult to keep his secret, as the story has been told and retold over the centuries.

Many, many years later, long after his death, Bishop Nicholas was made a saint. It was thought that he died on December 6, and this was made his feast day. Gradually this became a young people's festival, and grown-ups gave the children gifts in memory of St Nicholas.

In Europe and the United States the bishop's robe became a long, red, winter coat, and his mitre became a fur cap.

Some countries began to celebrate the feast day at Christmas. The Dutch name for St Nicholas was Sinter Claes, and this was soon adapted to Santa Claus.

Scandinavian countries imagined him travelling around with reindeer and a sleigh, and Father Christmas, as we know him, had arrived.

IN THE COUNTRY

SEASONAL SPOTTING

Give yourself points for the things on this page that you spot on country walks. (You could trace and colour the pictures too.)

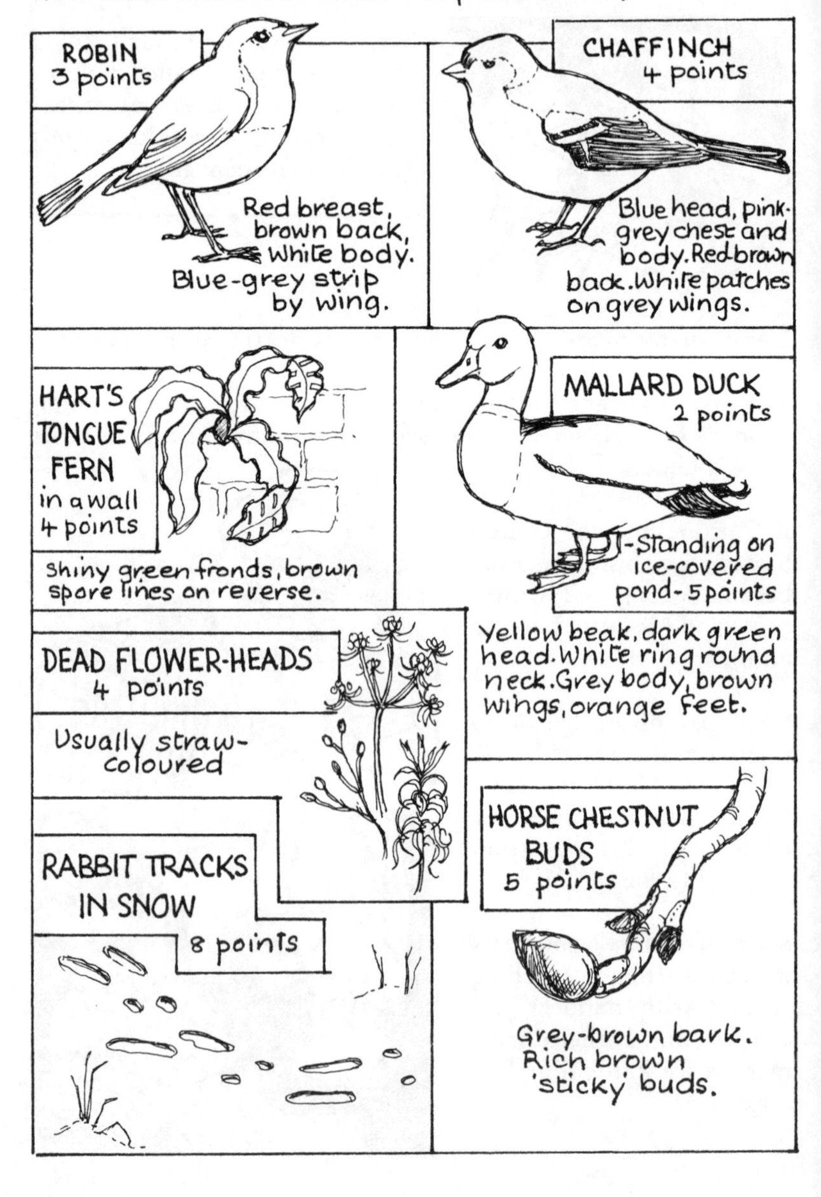

IN THE TOWN

SEASONAL SPOTTING

How many points can you award yourself by spotting these things?

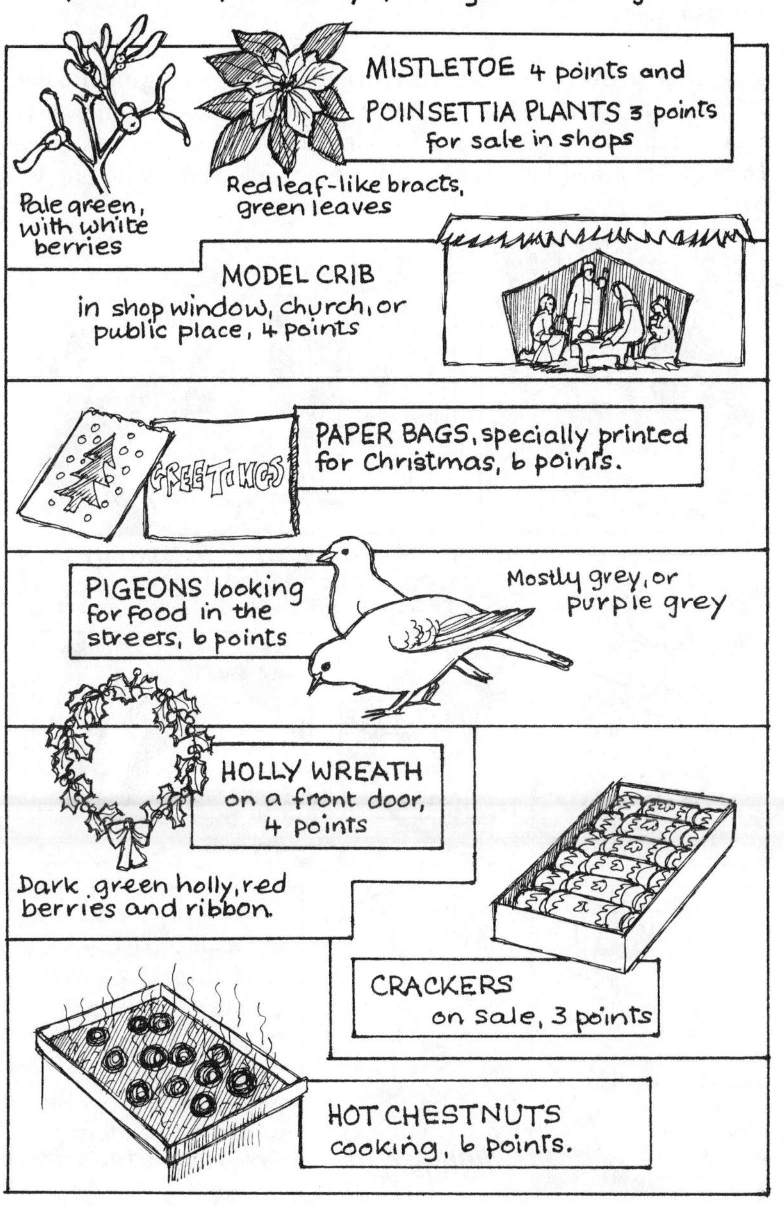

CHRISTMAS CRACKERS

Crackers are something very British – they were invented by an English man!

Just over a hundred and thirty years ago, a young man called Tom Smith owned, and worked in, a sweet shop in London. He was a man who was always looking for ways of expanding his trade, and he had his eyes open for new ideas, even when he was on holiday.

When Christmas came, Tom Smith sold sugared-almonds, each one wrapped in pretty paper, like the French ones.

Tom Smith was already busy. This time he was putting small toys and charms into his sweet packages. And he was still looking for new ideas...

It was only after about 2 years of experimenting that Tom Smith invented a friction strip that would CRACK! when pulled apart.

Now thousands are made and sold each year in Great Britain, and there is still a company in Tom Smith's name.

MAKE CRACKERS!

You will need:
Cardboard rolls, tissue paper, crepe paper. Trinkets or sweets. Cracker snaps - if possible (from craft shops). Glue, thread. Cut outs to decorate.

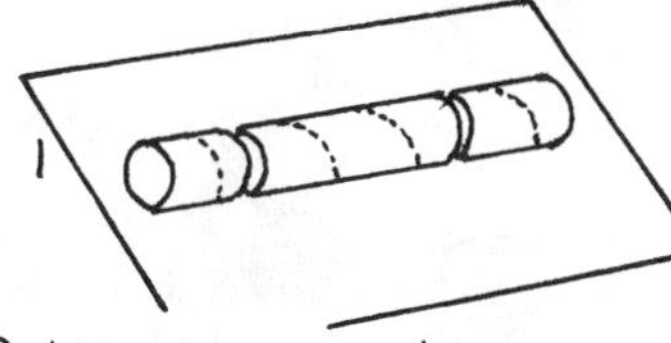

Put the tube on layers of tissue paper. Cut another tube in two and place at either end of longer tube. Roll paper round, and glue

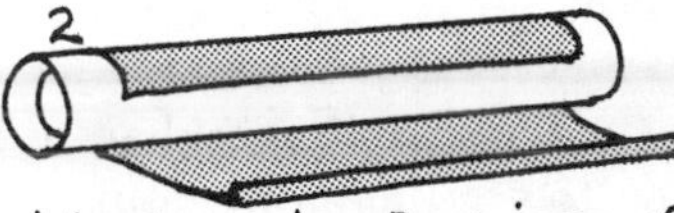

Wrap a shorter piece of crepe paper round the tubes, and glue.

Fill centre of tube with snap, motto, sweets etc

3

4

cut ends in pattern

With thread tie at each end of central tube. Remove two end tubes. Decorate with cut out shapes, pieces of doyley, glitter, etc.

BOXING DAY

The day after Christmas is the feast day of St Stephen.

Stephen is believed to be the first Christian martyr – that is, the first person to be killed because he was not afraid to declare that he was a follower of Jesus Christ. (Acts 7.54-60)

Many years later, Stephen was made a saint, and he is remembered particularly on December 26.

This day is also known as
BOXING DAY

On Boxing Day, servants, and those apprenticed to craftsmen, used to go to their masters and ask for gifts of money.

Every year they made 'boxes' in which to collect the money. These were hollowed out from clay and then baked. A slit was cut in the top of each box so that coins could be put in.

The earthenware 'boxes' had to be broken to get the money out.

Country servants often called these 'boxes' PIGGIES.

Have you ever called your money box a piggy bank?

MAKE YOUR OWN ‘PIGGIE’ to use as a money box

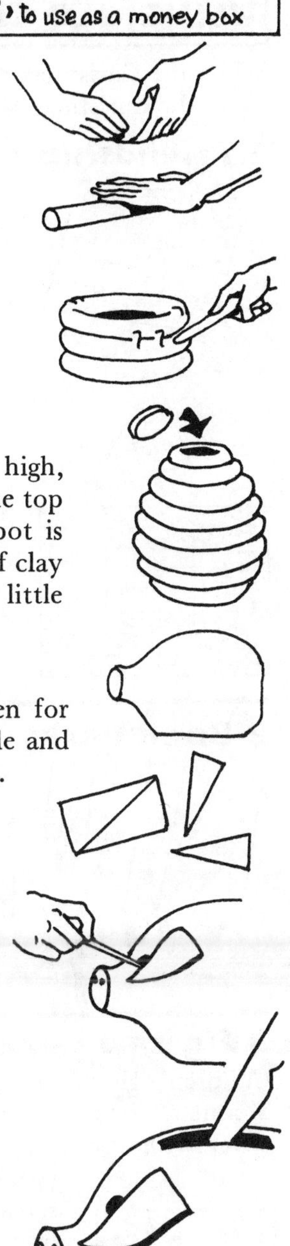

You will need modelling clay; it will last longer if you can use clay that does not need baking.

Roll a ball of clay and flatten it to a circle about 5cms (2ins) in diameter. Roll several long coils of clay and build up a pot shape on the circular base. Pull the end of a teaspoon or lolly stick across the coils to join them together firmly.

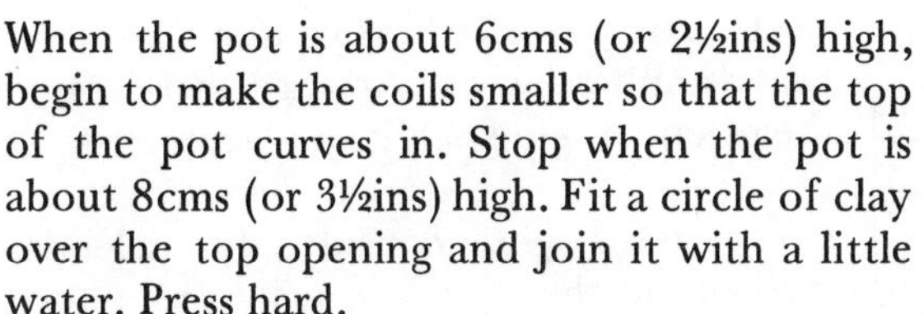

When the pot is about 6cms (or 2½ins) high, begin to make the coils smaller so that the top of the pot curves in. Stop when the pot is about 8cms (or 3½ins) high. Fit a circle of clay over the top opening and join it with a little water. Press hard.

Smooth the pot and leave it to harden for about an hour. Turn the pot on its side and press gently until it will stand on its side.

Press a piece of clay into a rectangle and cut in half diagonally.

Moisten one end of each triangle and stick to the pot for ears. Push a knitting needle through the clay for eyes and nostrils.

Cut a slit about 4cms (or 1½ins) long for coins.

Leave to dry, then paint and varnish your ‘piggie’.

USING OLD CHRISTMAS CARDS

When the Christmas decorations are taken down, do not throw away the Christmas cards. There are many uses for them.

1. Friendship calendar

Some shops and firms send 'a year at a glance' calendars to their customers. If you can obtain one of these, ask if you may cut off all the unnecessary lettering, leaving the dates of the year.

Stick this onto a much larger sheet of coloured paper. From your old Christmas cards, cut out all the signatures of your friends and relatives. Arrange these round the calendar and stick into place.

Every time you consult the calendar throughout the year, you will be reminded of your friends.

2. Bookmarks

Cut interesting strips from your old Christmas cards. Cover them with sticky transparent plastic to protect and strengthen them. Add a tassel made of wool.

3. Jig saw puzzle

Children's Homes and hospitals will be pleased to receive these. Mount a picture from a Christmas card on to thick card and cover with sticky transparent plastic. On the back, draw lines (straight or curved) and cut along them with scissors or a sharp knife. Put a coloured dot onto the back of each jig-saw piece, to distinguish it from others you make. Keep each puzzle in a separate envelope.

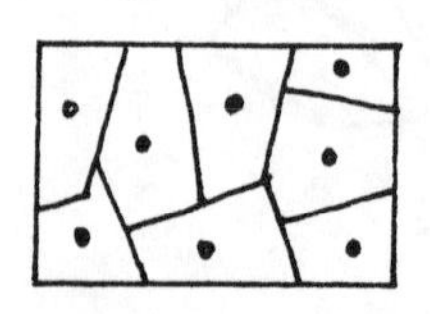

4. Mini-tops

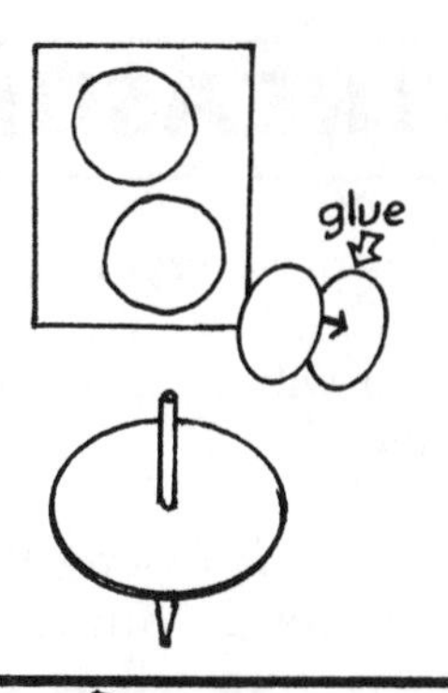

These are very simple to make, and will keep young children amused. From a gaily-coloured Christmas card cut two circles the same size and stick them together, coloured sides showing. Sharpen a used matchstick at one end and push it through the centre. Paint the matchstick to make it more attractive.

5. Memo sheets

Carefully cut off the white backs from Christmas cards. Punch a hole in the top of each card, and string about twenty together with a length of ribbon. Hang them in the kitchen to be used for shopping lists or notes.

6. Scrapbooks

These are a favourite way of using old cards. Cut the back off each card and stick the picture in the book. To make a record of those who sent the cards, copy the sender's name beside each as you stick it in.

Remember that hospitals and play-groups are usually pleased to have scrapbooks that you have made.

If you have no time to use your old Christmas cards, don't throw them in the dustbin. Play-group leaders, or teachers in Infant or First schools, will often be pleased to have them. Why not take them along to a play-group or school and ask?

TREASURE HUNT

Surprise everyone by organising a treasure hunt this Christmas!

You will need ten pieces of paper or card on which to write the clues.

Preparation Copy the clues on to the ten cards. Keep number 1, then fix the others in the places suggested. You may need to fix them with sellotape, but ask first! Make sure no one sees you hide them.

To play the game Read the first clue to all the players when they assemble for the game. This will tell them where to look for clue number 2. Tell them that no one must remove a clue; they may only read it. The rhyme on clue number 2 will give them an idea where the next clue is, and so on. The last clue will tell them to go back to the starting-place. The first one 'home' should be given a small prize as a reward!

Clue	Note
Find this clue somewhere you sit; get right down, look under it!	Keep this one to read out
Now find some glass in which you see a face reflected – you or me?	Fix this under an easy chair
Go to a room to wash your hands; this clue by white* enamel stands.	Fix this by a mirror
Now look for something that you hold when it is raining; it's in a fold.	Fix this by a washbasin
Get down, look up; this clue is where you sit to eat, but not a chair.	Fix this in the folds of an umbrella

**If you have a coloured wash basin, substitute the colour here.*

Clue	Where to fix
Go now to something used to cook; it isn't hard, but you must look!	Fix this under a table
This soft thing makes you sit at ease; just turn it over, if you please.	Fix this in a saucepan or on the cooker
When you come indoors at night, where do you put on the light?	Fix this under a cushion
Don't go outdoors, but you will see this clue is fastened on a tree!*	Fix this by the hall light switch
You've found the last, now go and claim, if you are first, the prize – and fame!	Fix this on the Christmas tree

*****_If you have no tree, substitute this verse:_
Don't go outdoors, this clue is seen
upon a piece of evergreen.
Then fix clue number 10 by holly or ivy, etc.

Decorate a small prize!

Lay a tube or roll of sweets on a piece of crepe or wrapping paper. This must be at least 8 cms longer than the sweets.

Cut a fringe on each end of the paper, then roll it round the sweets.

Tie cotton or wool tightly round at each end of the sweet tube. Now your prize will look really special!

CHRISTMAS PUZZLE PAGES

How many hidden toys can you find here? Trace the picture, then colour the marked shapes.

× yellow, • red, o green, * blue.

You could trace the picture on to a folded card and make a special Christmas card for a younger boy or girl. Write a greetings message inside.

Answers on page 128

Lots of people take family photographs at Christmas. Look at this one carefully and then decide which part below would match the marked square.

Answer on page 128

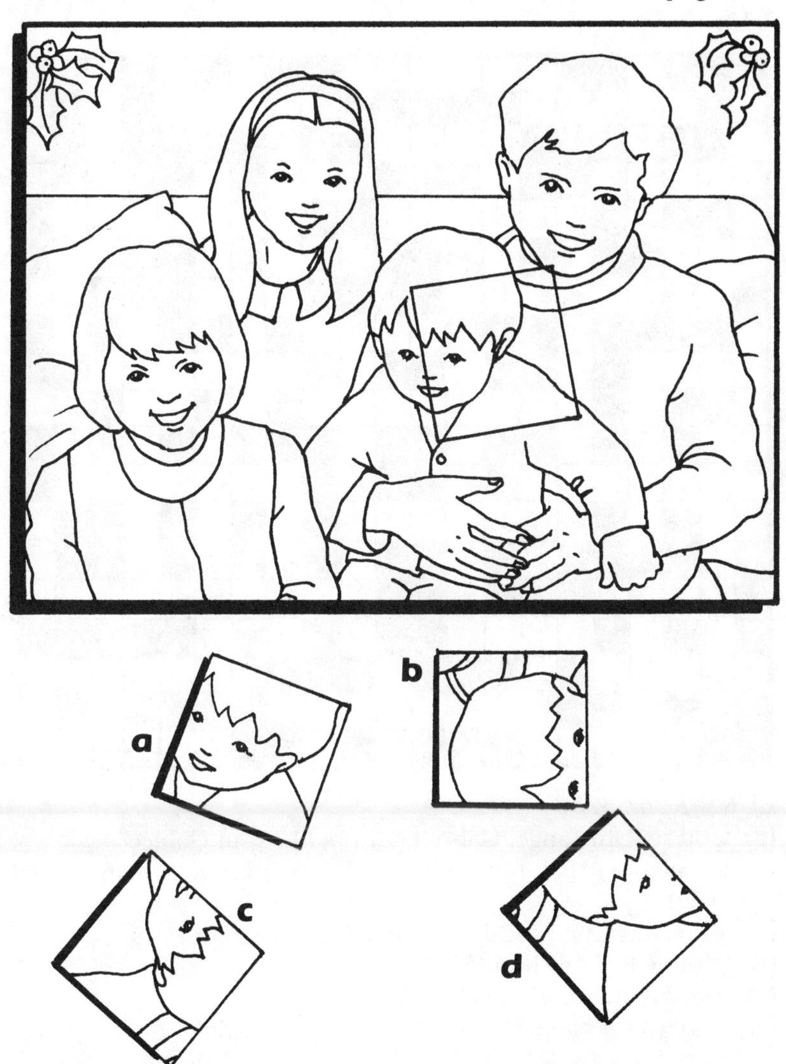

Make a similar puzzle for your friends by marking a square on a Christmas card and tracing it onto white card, with about three other possible squares.

CHRISTMAS CROSSWORD PUZZLE

Fill in the puzzle as you complete the sentences below. You will find them all in the Good News Bible, which is quoted on pages 7-13.

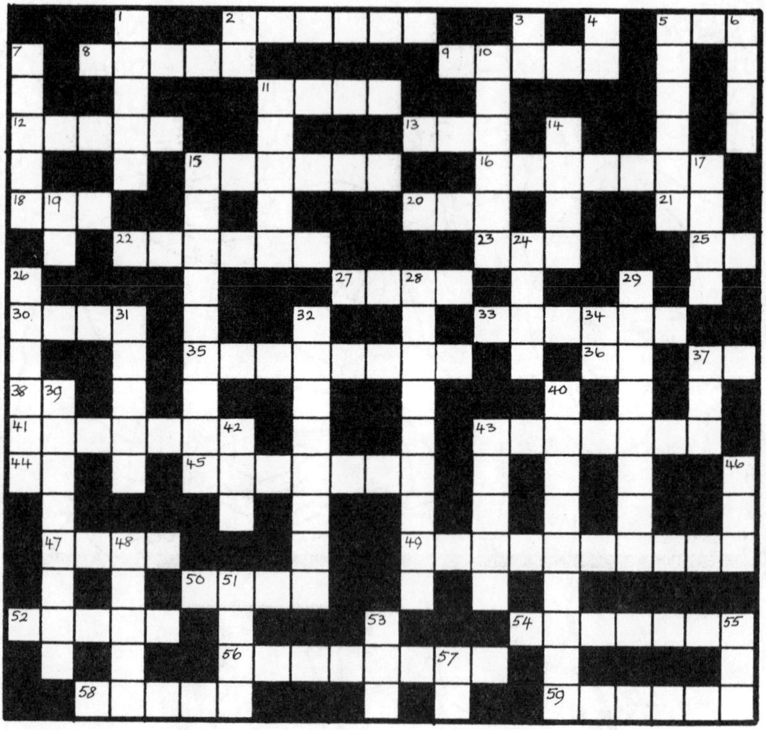

LUKE 1.26-33, 38

(a) God sent the angel Gabriel (21a) a (17d) in Galilee
(b) He had a (45a) for a girl (29d) in (56a) to a man named (15a)
(c) Mary was (59a) (39d) by the angel's message
(d) 'You will (24d) him (11d)'
(e) 'His kingdom will never (23a)!'
(f) 'May (38a) happen to me (3d) you have said'

LUKE 2.1-7

(a) (4d) that (51d) the Emperor Augustus ordered a census to be taken throughout the (7d) (33a)
(b) Joseph went there because he was a (49a) of (31d)

(c) He (6d) to (32d) with Mary, who was promised in marriage to him
(d) She gave (48d) to her first son, wrapped him in (26d) of cloth (37d) laid (53d) in a manger – there was (36a) room for them to stay in the inn

LUKE 2.8-20

(a) There were some (28d) in that part of the country
(b) (37a) angel (19d) the Lord (35a) to them and the (1d) of the Lord (58a) over them
(c) They were terribly afraid, (46d) the angel said to them, 'Don't be afraid! I am here with good news for you which will bring great joy to all the (10d)!'
(d) 'This very (55d) in David's town your Saviour was born – (22a) the Lord!'
(e) 'Glory to God in the highest (2a)'
(f) The shepherds said to one another, 'Let's (57d) to Bethlehem and (42d) this thing that has happened which the Lord has (30a) us'
(g) So they (43a) off and found Mary and Joseph and (5a) the (47a) lying in a manger
(h) (20a) who (52a) it were amazed
(i) The shepherds went back, singing (41a) to God

MATTHEW 2.1-12

(a) Soon afterwards, some men who (54a) the stars came from the (27a) to (15d)
(b) 'Where is the baby born to be the king of the (11a)?'
(c) '(25a) saw his (50a) when it came up (34d) the east'
(d) When King Herod heard about this, (2d) was very (9a) and (44a) was everyone else in Jerusalem
(e) 'This is what the (16a) wrote'
(f) So Herod called the visitors from the east to a (5d) meeting
(g) 'I (13a) may go and worship him'
(h) It stopped over the (8a) where the child was. They went into the (43d)
(i) They brought out their gifts of (14d), frankincense and (12a), and (40d) them to him
(j) God had warned them in a dream (18a) to go back to Herod

Answers on page 128

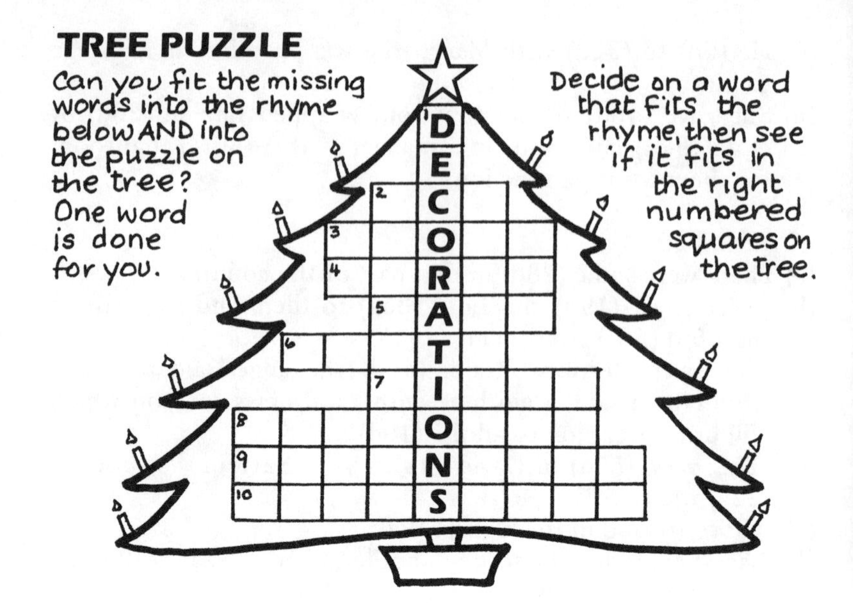

10__________ time will soon be here,
with 9_________ and cards;
the 5____ and 6_____ are put away,
and these our mother guards.
The 1 *DECORATIONS* bright and gay
are dancing to and fro;
it's warm indoors – outside perhaps
we'll have some 2___ and snow!
We'll have a 4_____, Christmas Eve,
with games and lots of fun;
then, tired, we'll go to bed at last,
when Christmas Eve is done.
That 7_____ we'll hang our stockings up,
and hope for sweets and toys –
Saint 8_________, or Santa Claus,
brings them for girls and boys.
With everyone at church next day
we'll hear the Christmas 3_____,
and all sing carols, glad to tell
of Jesus and his glory!

Answers on page 128

CHRISTMAS WORD SEARCH

All the words listed below have some connection with Christmas. Find them on the grid; the arrows show the direction in which to look. Every letter except X should be used at least once.

→

ASK
BED
BOY
GOD
HAT
ICE
GILT
GIRL
LOGS
OPEN
TUNE
YULE
TRADE
FAMILY
THRILL
WISE MEN

←

FUN
TOP
EATS
GOLD
MAIL
NUTS
TOYS
FRUIT
GOOSE
TABLE
CALENDAR
GREETINGS

↓

IVY
BABY
POEM
SACK
CHEER
FEAST
HOLLY
STORY
JOSEPH
ORANGE
WREATH
PANTOMIME

CUP
GIFTS
ROBIN
CANDLE
TURKEY

LORD
CAROL
PUDDING
SHEPHERDS

TEA
CRIB
JESUS
LIGHT
RED RIBBON
SANTA CLAUS

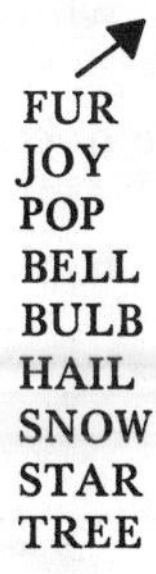

FUR
JOY
POP
BELL
BULB
HAIL
SNOW
STAR
TREE

ACTS
FOOD
MARY
ROOM
PARTY
PRESENTS

```
W I S E M E N X Y G I R L H X
R H A T X P L O G S A S Y O T
E X C E N O J P O T H R I L L
A S K L R E O C S F A M I L Y
T R A D E M S H L I A M O Y E
H S G N I T E E R G X P X O K
I C E A T P P E R X O A B X R
V P R C H A H R O P E N A N U
Y U L E X J C E L B A T B I T
F C R A D N E L A C B O Y B X
Y D R Y L R L S A L P M G O D
S R X I T E I R U U T I U R F
T T A L B R O B D S S M X A E
O H C M I L A D B E D E W N A
R S T A E G I P X O X O T G S
Y N U F X N H S T U N E O E T
X D L O G I L T E S O O G F A
```

QUIZ ON CHRISTMAS FOOD

After your Christmas dinner, your family might be glad to sit down and join in this quiz.

1. Mince pies were once oval in shape. Why?
2. Name one country where Christmas dinner is eaten in mid-summer.
3. Which of these was once popular as Christmas food: roast pelican, roast peacock, roast ostrich?
4. Mandarins, tangerines and clementines are all types of what fruit?
5. Name three important ingredients of mincemeat.
6. By what other name was Christmas pudding once known?
7. Whose parliament ordered that people did not *feast*, but *fast*, on Christmas Day?
8. From which country did we get our first turkeys?
9. Name one country where fish is a main Christmas dish.
10. What drink did the wassail bowl traditionally hold?

Answers on page 128

QUIZ ON CHRISTMAS CUSTOMS

How much does your family know about the customs of Christmas?

Answers on page 128.

1 Who was the German prince who introduced Christmas trees to Britain?

2 In what year did he do this?

3 What was the wassail bowl?

4 When is St Stephen's feast day?

5 Give two more names by which St Nicholas is known.

6 What did Boniface discover between the roots of an oak tree?

7 What was the medieval ring dance called?

8 When does Advent begin?

9 What was St Francis said to have introduced as a Christmas custom?

10 When is Epiphany, and who is particularly remembered on that day?

Can you rearrange these letters to make a famous book written by Charles Dickens?

CLASS TO ARMCHAIR

QUIZ ON THE CHRISTMAS STORY

In a quiet moment on Christmas Day try this quiz on your family.

1 Where was Mary living when the angel told her she would give birth to God's Son?

2 Why did Mary and Joseph have to travel to Bethlehem?

3 Why did they have to take refuge in a stable?

4 The shepherds were told to look for a baby wrapped in _____ lying in a _____; what and where?

5 Who was king of Judaea at the time when Jesus was born?

6 What made the wise men think that a new king of the Jews had been born?

7 When the wise men arrived in Jerusalem, where did they go first to look for the king?

8 What did the king of Judaea ask them to do?

9 Name the three gifts the wise men gave to the baby.

10 What did the wise men do after they had seen Jesus?

Answers on page 128

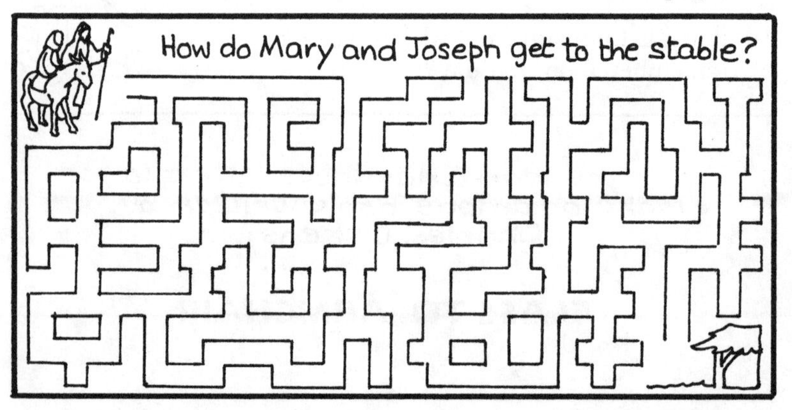

CHRISTMAS TEMPLATES

Make these shapes into templates by tracing them on to thin card and cutting them out. You can then draw round the card shapes as many times as you wish. The shapes will help you to make or draw many of the things suggested in this book. You can also use them to make up your own Christmas cards, friezes or decorations. Instructions for enlarging the shapes are given on page 127.

HOW TO ENLARGE PICTURES

Trace the template and draw a diagonal grid over the tracing

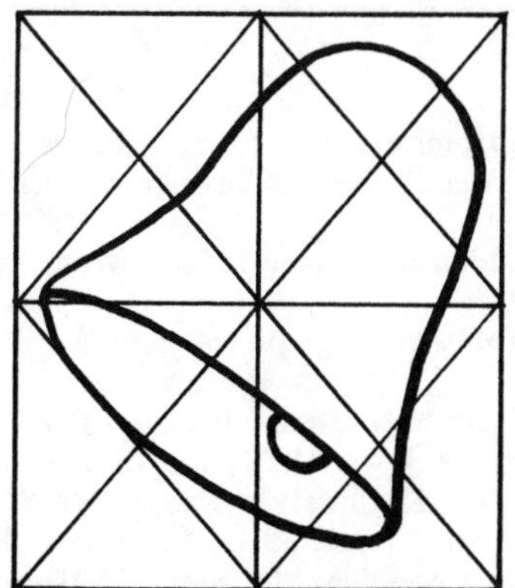

Make a similar grid on the paper or card on which you want to enlarge the drawing. (Make sure the rectangular outline is in scale.)

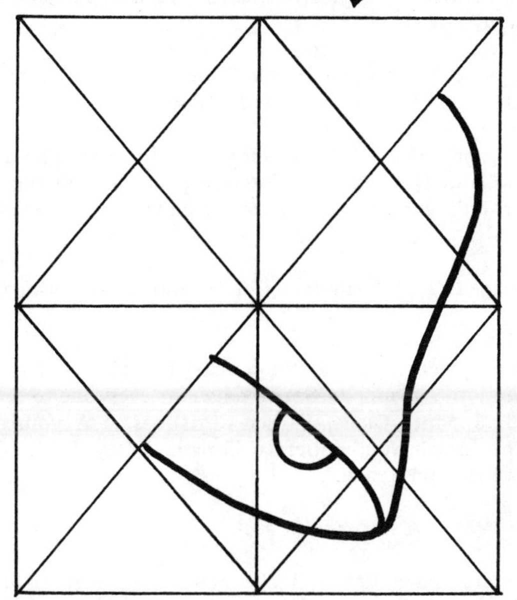

Enlarge the template one triangle at a time until you have completed the picture.

ANSWERS ARE HERE

Pantomimes (page 68) Babes in the Wood, Jack and the Beanstalk, Cinderella, Dick Whittington, Puss in Boots.

Hidden toys (page 116) Drum, teddy bear, kite, ball, boat, car, doll.

Family photograph (page 117) Piece c will fit.

Christmas crossword (page 118) Across: 2 Heaven, 5 Saw, 8 Place, 9 Upset, 11 Jews, 12 Myrrh, 13 Too, 15 Joseph, 16 Prophet, 18 Not, 20 All, 21 To, 22 Christ, 23 End, 25 We, 27 East, 30 Told, 33 Empire, 35 Appeared, 36 No, 37 An, 38 It, 41 Praises, 43 Hurried, 44 So, 45 Message, 47 Baby, 49 Descendant, 50 Star, 52 Heard, 54 Studied, 56 Marriage, 58 Shone, 59 Deeply. Down: 1 Glory, 2 He, 3 As, 4 At, 5 Secret, 6 Went, 7 Roman, 10 People, 11 Jesus, 14 Gold, 15 Jerusalem, 17 Town, 19 Of, 24 Name, 26 Strips, 28 Shepherds, 29 Promised, 31 David, 32 Register, 34 In, 37 And, 39 Troubled, 40 Presented, 42 See, 43 House, 46 But, 48 Birth, 51 Time, 53 Him, 55 Day, 57 Go.

Tree puzzle (page 120) 1 Decorations, 2 Ice, 3 Story, 4 Party, 5 Cake, 6 Gifts, 7 Night, 8 Nicholas, 9 Calendars, 10 Christmas.

Christmas food (page 122) 1 They were made to remind people of the manger. 2 Australia or New Zealand. 3 Roast peacock. 4 Oranges. 5 Suet, dried fruit, sugar. 6 Plum pudding. 7 Oliver Cromwell's. 8 America. 9 Italy, Finland. 10 Hot ale.

Name this boy (page 122) Little Jack Horner, and he was eating Christmas pie.

Christmas customs (page 123) 1 Prince Albert. 2 1841. 3 The bowl was passed round the lord's manor in Saxon days, for everyone to drink from. 4 December 26. 5 Santa Claus, Father Christmas. 6 A young fir tree. 7 A carol. 8 The fourth Sunday before Christmas Day. 9 The Christmas crib. 10 January 6; the wise men.

Book title (page 123) A Christmas Carol.

The Christmas story (page 124) 1 Nazareth. 2 To register in Joseph's ancestral home town. 3 There was no room in the inn. 4 Strips of cloth, or swaddling clothes; manger. 5 Herod. 6 They saw a star in the east. 7 The king's palace. 8 Report back to Herod after finding the baby. 9 Gold, frankincense, myrrh. 10 They returned home by another road.